Scott Foresman

Read Aloud

Anthology

Scott Foresman
is an imprint of

PEARSON

Glenview, Illinois • Boston, Massachusetts • Mesa, Arizona • Shoreview, Minnesota • Upper Saddle River, New Jersey

ISBN 13: 978-0-328-37872-2
ISBN 10:   0-328-37872-0

2 3 4 5 6 7 8 9 10 V031 17 16 15 14 13 12 11 10 09 08

Contents

Unit 4 One of a Kind

Unit 5 Cultures

Bugs for Breakfast

My first fried cricket. I closed my eyes and popped the golden brown nugget into my mouth. I munched slowly. It was crunchy, garlicky . . . and good! At first, I was a little nervous about going to an all-insect dinner at the science museum. But I soon got over it. After all, I wasn't the first person to eat insects. People in most cultures around the world have been eating them since ancient times, and they're still eating them today.

Why not? There are more insects on the planet than all other animals combined. In poor nations where the land is not suitable for raising cattle, insects are a useful source of protein. Insects are also cleaner than many animals we eat, and they taste great. Like any other food, insects need to be washed and cooked before they are served, and shouldn't be eaten straight out of your backyard.

The grasshopper is the most widely eaten insect in the world. Once you've tried one, it's easy to see why. Grasshoppers and crickets, which can be cooked many different ways, have a nutty taste. In Mexico, where over two hundred different species of insects are eaten, the grasshopper is tossed with a little onion and garlic and boiled or fried. Mashed grasshoppers are also mixed with beans and spread on tortillas. And long ago, North American Plains Indians ground grasshoppers into a paste to make fried cakes.

Many insects are eaten as larvae. The larva is the form some insects take after hatching from an egg. A larva usually looks like a short, fat, white worm, and though that may not sound appetizing, they're often considered a rare treat. Because of their high fat content they are sometimes tossed into cooking pots instead of butter.

Insects are not just eaten as a main course; they also make a tasty snack. In Columbia, leaf-cutter ants are roasted like peanuts and served in movie houses instead of popcorn. They taste like crispy bacon. In some parts of Africa, termites are scooped up and eaten just like a fistful of peanuts. Southern Africans also enjoy the delicious mopanie caterpillar, which is known as "the snack that crawl."

Are you ready for dessert? How about a sweet, sticky honeypot ant? They are found in Australia and the western United States. You grab a live one by the head and bite off the large globe of honey that's stored in its abdomen. The brown ones are called cola ants, and the golden ones are called butter ants. Both are delicious.

Insects are so plentiful it's silly not to use them as a food source, especially when hunger is a problem in so many countries. A few hundred years ago, early settlers in America often ate grasshoppers when other food was hard to find. But as countries become industrialized, more and more people reject the idea of eating bugs. Today, some people are trying to introduce the eating of bugs by writing recipe books and serving delicious insect dishes in restaurants.

Although you can't go out and order a cricketburger at a fast-food place yet, you should start thinking about insects as a food. Sometime in the future, when an ant crawls across your arm or you hear a cricket chirping in the woods, you might say to yourself, "What's for dinner?" So don't get butterflies in your stomach when you think about eating insects—or if you do, try them fried.

New Kid

BY Dori Hillestad Butler

Kayla hated being the new kid. She hated being stared at. The boy who sat across from her had been staring at her since she sat down.

Kayla was about to tell him to take a picture, it lasts longer, when suddenly he said, "Nice shirt."

Kayla glanced at her AAU Junior Olympics shirt.

"I've got one just like it at home," the boy said.

"You were at the Junior Olympics?" Kayla asked. What were the odds of her running into another Junior Olympics competitor at her new school?

"Yup. Basketball," he said proudly. "What's your sport?"

"Table tennis," Kayla replied.

"Oh." He rolled his eyes.

Kayla had seen that reaction before. She crossed her arms. "I suppose you think table tennis isn't a *real* sport," she said.

"Well, you have to admit Ping-Pong just isn't as physical as basketball." Kayla cringed when he said Ping-Pong. "It's a rec room game," he went on. "Like pool. Or checkers."

Kayla wanted to wipe the smirk off this kid's face. "Maybe you and I should play a match sometime," she said.

He smiled as though this was the most ridiculous thing he'd ever heard. "You're challenging *me?*" he asked.

He turned to the boy who sat behind him. That boy raised his eyebrows as if Kayla had to be an idiot for challenging the other boy to *anything*.

Kayla ignored him. "Are you up to a challenge?" she asked the first boy.

"Name the time and place," he said.

"My house. After school today," Kayla said.

"You got it," he said.

Later Kayla found out the boy's name was Michael Savitch. She also found out Michael didn't just play basketball. He played practically everything.

"Do you really think you can beat him?" a short girl with glasses asked Kayla. Her name was Holly.

"Maybe," Kayla said.

"Could we watch?" asked Holly's friend Mindy.

"Sure," Kayla said.

Holly and Mindy invited Kayla to eat lunch with them. They introduced her to Jessica. Jessica introduced her to Paula. Paula introduced her to Sara. And each time, Kayla was introduced as "the girl who's going to beat Michael Savitch at table tennis."

"Wow!" Each girl looked at Kayla with admiration.

Was Michael really that good? Kayla wondered. What if she made a fool of herself? What if Michael actually beat her? Would Holly, Mindy, Jessica, Paula, and Sara still want to be her friends?

Kayla's mom looked surprised when Kayla came home with nine people that day. "We're going to play some table tennis," Kayla said.

Kayla grabbed a bag of apples from the fridge and headed down to the basement. The other kids clattered down the stairs behind her.

"We'll have to move some boxes," Kayla said. "We're not quite moved in yet."

"No problem," Michael said. He and the boys picked up the boxes at one end of the table and set them around the corner. Kayla and the girls moved the boxes from the other end of the table.

The boys stopped when they had cleared a six-foot area behind the table. "You need to clear all the way to the wall," Kayla said.

"What for?" one of the boys asked. "Are we here for Ping-Pong or cheap labor?"

"*Table tennis,*" Kayla said through gritted teeth. "And I need lots of room to play."

"OOOOO," said the boys. But they grudgingly moved the rest of the boxes. Kayla crawled under the table and opened the box labeled table tennis supplies.

When everything was set up, Michael asked, "Could we warm up a little?"

"Sure," Kayla said.

The girls lined up along one side of the table. The boys lined up along the other. The only sound in the room was the *plink plunk* of the ball as it bounced from court to court.

If Michael had any tricks, he didn't show them during their easy volleys. Kayla didn't show hers either.

"You ready to play?" Kayla asked.

Michael nodded. He won the serve, and the game began. Michael wasn't bad. But Kayla was better.

Michael's main problem was not knowing when to go for the kill shot. He also got confused when Kayla gave him a loop shot.

Kayla had Michael running all over his court. The kids who were watching the game had to move away from the table so they wouldn't get plowed over. Kayla won the first game 21 to 7. The girls cheered and the boys groaned.

"That's O.K.," Michael panted. His damp hair was plastered to his forehead. "I'm warmed up now."

Sure you are, Kayla thought to herself. She hadn't even shown him her sidespin yet.

The second game was over even faster than the first. Kayla won 21 to 5. The girls jumped up and down, clapping. "She won!" Holly cried. "She beat Michael Savitch!" Mindy yelled.

Kayla bounced the ball on the table a few times and looked over at Michael. "Still think table tennis isn't a physical game?" she asked.

Michael wiped his face with the bottom of his shirt. He didn't say anything.

"Should we try another nonphysical game?" Kayla asked. "Maybe eightball?"

Michael eyed the pool table wearily. "Give me a few days to practice up first," he said.

Kayla smiled. She'd made her point. Good thing, too. She was awful at pool.

The Story of Money

BY CAROLYN KAIN

Exchange of goods

Long ago, people had to wander from place to place searching for food. But about 10,000 years ago, people found that if they collected seeds and planted them, a crop would grow. They also had to tame wild animals. Now they had a permanent food supply, and there was no need to wander. Gradually, small villages grew up.

These people made baskets, sacks, and pots for storing their food. They also made tools to dig the land, harvest their crops, and build their houses. Over the years, they discovered that some people were better at making pots, while others were better at making baskets or hoes. The pot-maker might exchange a pot for some food, or a tool. Someone who made an ax might feel it was worth four pots because the ax took longer to make. The people must have agreed upon a fair way of exchanging items.

The marketplace

People carefully chose the place where they settled. Villages often grew up where there was good soil for growing crops, or plenty of clay for making pots, or reeds for making baskets. As a result, some villages might have more grain than they needed or more pots than they needed. If the people could not trade goods within the village, they took them to a marketplace.

Here people from several villages met to exchange their goods for items they needed. This system of trading is called barter. Often it works well, but sometimes there are problems, as in the following example.

Four people, each with something to barter, arrive at the marketplace. One has fish and wants a spear, another has a spear and needs grain, a third has grain and would like a pot, and the fourth has a pot but wants a spear. Unfortunately, no one gets anything.

Precious objects

It became obvious that a system of exchange does not always work, so people in different parts of the world developed ways of solving this problem. Certain objects were agreed upon as being precious. If you sold something, you received a number of these objects. If you then wanted to buy something, you would pay with them. These objects were used as money.

In some Pacific Islands, people used stone wheels for buying and selling goods. Cattle, tools, weapons, packets of salt, cacao beans, glass beads, and bricks of pressed tea have all been used as money. In parts of Africa, people used cowrie shells. But when traders arrived from India, they would not sell their goods for cowrie-shell money. In India, thousands of these shells were washed up on the beaches, so to the Indians, this kind of money was worthless.

The first coins

As trade in different parts of the world increased, it became necessary to find something that was precious to everyone. Gold and other rare metals were already valued for their beauty.

In Babylon, chips from gold and silver bars were weighed and used as money. In Egypt, gold and silver bands were weighed on scales using stone or bronze weights in the shapes of animals. These animals had formerly been used as money. The first coins were made about 2,700 years ago.

In China, the first coins were called *cash*. In Greece, each small coin was marked with its weight. Later, important gods and rulers were pictured on the coins. Roman bronze coins pictured a cow. This reminded people that coins were valuable in the same way as cattle.

The Great Tulip Trade

BY BETH WAGNER BRUST

Anna loved tulips. She loved their round shape and bright colors and slim green leaves.

But in Holland in 1636, *everyone* loved tulips! That made tulips worth more than gold and diamonds. More than almost anything.

One spring morning, Anna saw her father cutting tulips. People wanted the bulbs the most.

"Stop, Papa!" said Anna.

"Sorry, Birthday Girl," he said. "My bulbs in the ground grow bigger and better without the flower."

"Please, let me have some tulips for my birthday," begged Anna.

"Very well," he said. "You may choose eight since you are now eight."

"Thank you!" said Anna.

First, she chose two red ones. Then two yellow ones. A purple one. A pink-and-white-striped one. A red one with yellow edges that looked like flames. Then her favorite tulip. The rarest tulip of all, the Semper Augustus.

Anna put all the tulips in her wheelbarrow and pushed it to their cottage. She planted them in a window box.

Soon she saw a farmer bringing his sheep and cows to market.

"What pretty tulips!" he said. "I'll trade you for a red tulip. And a yellow one," he said. The farmer thought he could sell the tulips for more than his sheep and cows.

"Sorry, they're not for sale," said Anna. "They are my birthday present."

"I'll give you a lamb," said the farmer.

"No, thank you," said Anna.

He held up another lamb. "I'll give you two lambs, a cow, and a puppy."

Anna felt bad. The tulips were her present. But with lambs, her family could spin the wool to make into cloth. With a cow, they could have fresh milk, butter, and cheese. And the puppy would grow bigger and protect their tulip field. Besides, Anna would still have six tulips left.

"All right, I'll trade," she said.

A while later, a peddler and his wife stopped their wagon.

"What lovely flowers!" called the peddler. "I'll trade you some pots and pan for the pink-striped one."

The peddler knew that he could sell the tulip for more than his pots and pans.

"No, thank you," said Anna.

"Add the red one," said the man, "and you may have this warm wool rug."

Anna looked at the rug. She looked at her red tulip. Their stone floor was cold. A rug would be nice. Four tulips would be left. She would still have her favorite, the very rare Semper Augustus.

"All right," she said. Anna took the pots and pans.

At noon, an artist walked by. "What a picture-perfect tulip!" he said.

"Thank you," said Anna.

"Would you trade that purple tulip for a painting?" he asked. He knew it would be worth more than twenty paintings.

"No, thank you," said Anna. "They are my birthday present."

"Painted flowers never wilt," said the artist. He turned his board around. Anna gasped. She had never seen such a pretty picture!

Anna thought about the bare cottage walls.

"I will trade," she said.

The artist gave Anna the painting.

"Happy birthday," he said.

Soon a wagon heaped with furniture pulled up. "I must buy that flamed tulip!" called the furniture maker.

"It is not for sale," said Anna.

"I'll trade you this cabinet for it," the man said.

"No," said Anna.

"The cabinet, a dining table, *and* six chairs?" he asked.

Anna knew they could use a cabinet. And they needed a bigger table. But NO! These three tulips were her last!

"Sorry," said Anna. "No trade."

The man's face turned as red as the tulip.

"Impossible!" he cried. "Give me the yellow one, too, and I'll give you all that *and* a bed with a feather mattress."

A real bed! Now *that* was special! Her family would sleep on a bed instead of on hard boards.

"Yes," said Anna.

"Here comes Papa!" shouted Anna's brother.

Anna looked at her window box. Oh dear! Only one tulip was left. What would Papa say?

Suddenly, a coach pulled up. "Ooooooohh!" squealed a woman. I *must* have that tulip!"

The mayor leaned out the window. "Girl, how much for that flower?"

"It's not for sale," said Anna.

"Nonsense!" he said. "My lady wants that flower."

Anna looked at her father.

"Where are your other tulips?" asked Papa.

Anna's brother spoke first. "Anna traded them for a table, pots and pans, a painting and a puppy, a bed and a rug, a cabinet and a cow, two lambs, and six chairs!"

Papa stepped back. "For seven tulips you got all that?" he said.

Anna nodded. "But this is my favorite. I'm keeping it for my birthday."

"I'll trade this gold necklace for it," the mayor shouted.

Anna shook her head.

"*And* this diamond bracelet *and* these gold coins!"

Anna shook her head.

The mayor looked ready to explode. "The jewelry, the money, and a big house!" he shouted. "All for one tulip."

Anna's father took her aside. "Am I silly not to want to trade?" asked Anna.

"No," said her father. "It is your choice. But today, your rare tulip is worth a big house. Tomorrow, no one may want tulips. They may be worth nothing at all."

Anna nodded. She thought she understood.

"Well?" asked the mayor.

"Is it mine?" asked his wife.

Anna put the Semper Augustus in a clay pot.

The mayor reached out.

Anna didn't move. "I will not trade my very last birthday tulip. It is a gift from my father. That makes it worth more to me than anything else."

Author's Note

In Holland in the 1600s, people loved tulips. Some people bought tulip bulbs with Dutch money called florins. Others traded their animals, jewelry, gold, and land for tulips. This made the price keep going up. A tulip bulb cost a hundred florins one day. The next day, it was worth much more. People saw buying and selling tulips as a way to get rich.

The Semper Augustus really was the most rare and expensive tulip. One sold for 4,600 florins, a coach, and a pair of horses.

In the winter of 1637, tulip mania hit its high point. Then the prices dropped like a rock and tulips were worth next to nothing. Many people lost all of their money, including the famous Dutch artist Rembrandt.

All this for an ugly little bulb that looked like an onion but turned into the loveliest of flowers!

This Is a Park Your Community Built

BY PATRICIA WALSH

What if there is an open space in your town, but it has nothing but weeds and dried-up grass, and maybe some unpicked-up trash scattered here and there? What if there are no parks in this neighborhood where the open land is located? What if there is no place for children to play and no place for moms and dads to take their babies for a walk? What would you do? Would you plan to build a park?

People in towns all across the nation have built parks for their neighborhoods. Neighborhood groups in these towns saw open space, and they said, "A community park is what we need here, and we are the ones to build it."

But parks can't be built without funds. The first thing each neighborhood group had to do was raise money. Some groups needed money to buy the land for the park. Other groups needed money to buy the materials and equipment for the park.

What would you do to raise money so that you could build a new park? Here is what the people in Winfield, Kansas, did. They put on special events that included parties. They had a Hawaiian luau party and a New Year's Eve party. These parties were fundraisers. People paid money, called a donation, to come to the parties. The money they gave was used to build their new park.

The people in this town also "sold" pieces of the park. With a donation, you could buy one wooden picket for a new picket fence. Your name would be put on the picket. Then all the pickets would be put together to make the new fence for the new park. Or with your donation, you could buy one brick for the new walkway. Your name would be engraved on the brick. Then all the bricks would be laid together to make the new walkway for the new park.

There is a park in Silver City, New Mexico, and another one in Evanston, Illinois, that have the word *penny* in their names. They are called Penny Playground and Penny Park. Why do you think these parks are called "Penny"? The names come from events that the people organized to raise money for the new parks. School children were asked to collect and donate pennies to help build these parks. Thousands and thousands of pennies were raised. So what better name than Penny Park for a playground built with the money raised from children's pennies?

Having a name for the park before you actually build it helps spread the word about your project so that people know about it. That way they can help by donating money. The people in Las Cruces, New Mexico, had a naming contest. They asked children to come up with a name for their new park. The winning name was Unidad Park. *Unidad* means "unity" in Spanish. The contest judges thought this was the right name for a park that would bring lots of people together.

The children of Pell City, Alabama, chose the name for their new community park. They called it Kids Kastle. If you think there is a castle in the park, you are correct. There is a large wooden castle to climb on and hop off of, right in the middle of the park. What would you name your new park?

So let's see, what do you have so far for you new park? You have open space in which to build it. You have a name for it. You have lots of ideas about what it should look like and what kinds of things you might want to put there. And you have money from fundraising to make your ideas become real.

Now it is time to make some final decisions. What exactly should be in your park? Let's look at other parks to help us brainstorm some ideas. In Penny Park in Evanston, Illinois, there is a sandbox, swings for babies, and a tire swing for the bigger kids. There are lots of balance beams to walk along and monkey bars to hang from. There are benches and picnic tables too. Tables are a good idea. Besides having a picnic on a table, kids can use it as a place to do their homework on warm days after school.

Penny Playground in Silver City, New Mexico, is filled with things to climb on, slides to slide on, and bridges to cross. And just like the park in Pell City, Alabama, they have a castle to climb on as well. Here is another important idea for a park: trees. Trees will give you shady spots on summer days. And don't forget colorful flowers to make the place look beautiful.

Some parks are created around a theme. A theme in a park means that all the structures have a similar look or idea. A theme can add extra amusement to your park too. Here is an example. The children's park in Lubec, Maine, looks like a fishing village, just like the real town of Lubec. Their park has ships and a lighthouse, just like Lubec. Lobster fishing is an important job in Lubec, so artists in the community made a huge sculpture of a lobster trap with a giant lobster sculpture inside. This pretend lobster and its trap are right in the middle of the park for everyone to enjoy.

The children and adults in Winfield, Kansas, got together to brainstorm for ideas for their new park. Guess what they came up with. Their park has a giant castle, a Viking ship, the Statue of Liberty, a space shuttle, a farm combine, and a horse and wagon. It also has little stores that look just like the big stores in the real town of Winfield. The children can have lots of fun pretending in this park.

Remember Kids Kastle Park in Pell City, Alabama? It has a Tot Lot. The Tot Lot is a playground for little children from 2 to 5 years old. It has a tot-sized rainbow slide and a miniature maze. The moms and dads are happy that the planners remembered benches too, so that they have a place to sit down and watch while their children play.

Now take all your ideas and make a drawing. A drawing of all your ideas is called a design. The design will be your plan. Everyone who has lent their help so far will want to collaborate on this plan. The plan is what everyone will use later to work together to build the park.

Here are a few questions to get you started on your plan. Where will the equipment go? Where will you put the little buildings and the big buildings? What about the picnic tables? Should they go under the trees? And where will the walkways begin and where will they end? When your drawing is done, you will see everyone's ideas come together.

So let's see. How far are you in your project for a park so far? You have open space. You have a name. You have lots of ideas that came from your brains all working together. You have money from fundraising to make your ideas real. And now you have a design plan in place for the open space, showing exactly what will be there and where it will go.

Choosing the materials for your new park is the next step. Will your playground be built with wood? Will it be built with metal or plastic? Think about what should be underfoot on the ground. A park needs something soft for kids to land on when they jump down from the swings. You might put sand, wood chips, or shredded rubber made from old recycled tires on the ground of your new park.

What do you need next? Volunteers! On construction day, lots of people, young and old, some with building skills and some with no skills at all, will come together to build the park. College students, high school students, middle school and elementary students can all help. Firefighters, policemen, and even the mayor can help. Teachers, doctors, neighbors, and friends can all help. What will all these volunteers do? They will saw wood, hammer nails, pour concrete, drill holes, tighten screws, paint the castle, spread wood chips, and hang the swings.

It's a big job. How big? Well, it took 779 volunteers to help build a community park in San Jose, California. The volunteers worked for five days. The workers used 1,100 tools. They cut and sawed 4 miles of lumber. They poured lots of concrete, hauled 36 tons of sand, pounded 300 pounds of nails, and screwed and tightened 30,000 screws and bolts. And the food committee served 1,500 meals. That's a lot of work!

Who did this work? Everyone! Young children rubbed the screws in soap bars to make them twist easily into the wood. Older brothers and sisters sanded wood to make it smooth. Adults rolled the wheelbarrows to spread the sand and wood chips in just the right place. Your park project will rise right before your eyes, too, just as it did for all those volunteers in San Jose, California.

And what will you do at the end of the final day of construction, when the park is all done? You will celebrate, of course! You will have a grand-opening party. People will hug and whoop and laugh and jump all around. But don't just stand back and admire your creation. Get in there and play, because . . . this is a park your community built.

Dorothy's Dream Role

BY ALYCIA RIANT

The activity room of Caleb Venture elementary school seemed to be filling up fast. Students were seated on the floor around the room, some alone, some in groups of two or three or four. Many had their backpacks with them, which they used as backrests or elbow supports. Some of them were reading, and some were playing electronic games that they held in their hands and peered at as intently as if they were about life and death. Maybe some of the games *were* about life and death.

Over the room there was a hum of conversation, laughter, and students calling across to each other. Dorothy Gentry was trying hard to read in the midst of all this. It was a chapter book in a series that she was enjoying hugely. But she was finding it difficult to concentrate with all the noise and activity. Then she noticed that Mrs. McLean and Mr. Ramiro were climbing the steps to the stage. Carefully, she placed her construction-paper-with-yarn-tassel bookmark that her best friend Amy had made for her at the beginning of the year (as she had made one for Amy), closed the book, and slid it into her backpack.

All around her, students were beginning to notice and to quiet down. There were announcements coming that they really wanted to hear.

Two days before, Mrs. McLean and Mr. Ramiro had held tryouts for the upcoming school play. Not the entire third grade, perhaps, but almost all of the students had shown up. Word was around that these teachers made rehearsals a lot of fun. And, of course, you had the opportunity to be onstage in front of your family and friends, with everyone applauding like crazy. How cool was *that?*

This year's show was *Cinderella*. It was an old and familiar story, but everybody liked it. "But this year," Mr. Ramiro had explained, "we're going to do something a little different. Obviously, this stage isn't big enough for a grand ballroom, so we're going to have dancers waltz down the aisles and do a little dance down in front of the stage, in the orchestra pit. Though we don't have an orchestra, of course, just me, on piano."

"So, many of you will be dancers at the ball," Mrs. McLean had added. "Now, don't worry. Mr. Ramiro is going to teach you some very simple dance steps that you can all do. And look graceful and wonderful, I'm sure," she had concluded, grinning.

They had had readings after that. One by one students clumped up the hollow wooden stairs to the stage, stood in the center close to the front, announced their names, and then read lines off of photocopied pages that Mrs. McLean handed out. One thing Dorothy couldn't figure out was why none of the pages had Cinderella's part. They were all Ugly Stepsisters or Evil Stepmothers or Fairy Godmothers—or Princes or Kings, or Pages, of course. But how on earth were they going to be able to choose a good Cinderella when they never actually heard anyone read Cinderella's lines?

But Dorothy had read. Her tryout part was one of the Ugly Stepsisters—and she actually got laughs from a few students when she made a kind of ugly face at the end. That made her feel good.

How did she do? She didn't know. Nobody knew. That was what today was about, to announce the parts—Mr. Ramiro had called it "cast list"—before they had their first rehearsal.

Cinderella. Her dream role. Dorothy wanted to play Cinderella so badly, she—well, she couldn't think of an adequate description, but badly. It *was* her dream role, in fact. These last two nights since the tryouts she'd had a dream in which she—as Cinderella—had gathered up her beautiful full skirts and had sped down that long, curving flight of marble steps, only to discover— *Why, what's wrong with my right slipper? (Gasp!) It's gone! I've lost my slipper, that dainty slipper of sparkling glass! My Fairy Godmother will be furious!* Dorothy had to play the role of Cinderella, she felt. She just *had* to!

Her mother, also, had gotten caught up in the enthusiasm. When Dorothy had come home after the tryouts and told her mother how well she had read, Mrs. Gentry had just beamed.

"Oh, darling, you'll make a wonderful Cinderella! I can just see you, up there on that stage! A gown—you'll need a gown. I wonder if the school is going to furnish costumes, or—you know, I've got that curtain fabric in the trunk downstairs, that would sew up—no, wait. My old lace tablecloth. It's got some candlewax stains, but if we put them on the inside . . ."

Dorothy scarcely had a chance to say anything when her mother got like this.

"We'll have to make sure, won't we," Mrs. Gentry had continued, laughing, "that your feet are very clean—if the Prince is going to put your shoe on. Or wait, maybe you should have dirty feet, since Cinderella sits in the ashes all the time . . . ."

"Time," Mr. Ramiro was saying from the stage. "It's time to announce our cast list for this year's class play, *Cinderella*, Now, some of you are going to get excited, but please keep your enthusiasms under control until I finish reading the whole list. Otherwise, people won't be able to hear. Okay? Here we go. Since everyone is so anxious to know who the star of our show is going to be—well, no, we don't have any stars here. But of course, somebody has to play the title character, and that person is—

Dorothy Gentry. Was that what he said, or was that what she heard, because she wanted so much? No, wait—

"That person," announced Mr. Ramiro, "is—Ginger Weiss."

It can't be! Ginger Weiss? Dorothy wanted to shout, "Stop!" Wanted to stand up and tell Mr. Ramiro, "You've got it all wrong! It's supposed to be me!"

But, of course, she remained seated on the tiled floor of the activity room, and she kept her mouth shut. But now she was finding it hard to concentrate. For now there seemed to be growing in her ears a buzzing noise that threatened to drown out all other sounds in the room. And so she hardly heard Mr. Ramiro continue his announcements:

"Ugly Stepsister Flora, Mary Thorp . . . Ugly Stepsister Fauna, Harmony Withers . . . Fairy Godmother, Dorothy Gentry . . . Prince Charming, Will Simms . . . Page . . . ."

Dorothy put her hands over her ears, but that couldn't stop the buzzing. Then she used one palm to feel her forehead. She felt hot. Maybe she was running a fever. She was sure her face had turned an embarrassing shade of red.

Finally she noticed students starting to move from their places, to pick up their backpacks and get to their feet. In a daze, she did the same, scurrying for the exit as she barely heard Mr. Ramiro's voice over the growing hum of conversations: "Five minutes, everybody. Then we'll get back together and have our first read-through . . . ."

Dorothy dashed down the hallway (ignoring the "Don't Run" rule) until she reached her cubby outside Mrs. McLean's classroom. There she threw her backpack on the floor and leaned against the wall of cubbies, arms stiff and trembling as she gasped for breath. The thought came to her: *Mother! She'll be so disappointed!*

It was in that position that Mrs. McLean found her, moments later.

"We've only got five minutes, Dorothy. You can't afford to hang around . . ."

"I think—I think—" Dorothy managed to croak out, "I'm not going back in there, Mrs. McLean. I think I have to go home now."

"Why, whatever's the matter? Are you not feeling well? Do you need to see the nurse?"

"No, no—I'll be all right."

"Are you sure? I can't let you go, anyway, because we've rescheduled the busses to accommodate the rehearsal, and—"

"No! I'm sorry, Mrs. McLean, I just . . . ."

But Dorothy's voice faded out as Mrs. McLean peered earnestly into her face.

"I just came back to get my sweater—it's a bit drafty in there—but I think we can take a couple of minutes to talk. Why don't you tell me what's wrong?"

Dorothy had regained some control of herself. She realized she had been foolish, but she felt safe telling Mrs. McLean the truth.

"I wanted—to be Cinderella."

Mrs. McLean smiled. "So did all the other girls in there."

"But I *really*—"

"You know, Dorothy, maybe you set your goal a little high. Not that there's anything wrong with wanting to play Cinderella. Not that there's anything wrong with *really* wanting to play Cinderella. But if you set your goal—no, not lower—but *differently*—"

"Like what?"

"There's an old story about a man who was thought to be an archery champion. Everyone who went to visit him marveled at the number of bulls-eyes displayed all over. Until someone discovered his secret: he'd shoot the arrow first and then paint the target around it."

"I don't understand. Was he cheating?"

"Okay, bad example. Suppose if—instead of having your goal "I want to play Cinderella," you had your goal "I want to do a good job in the play.""

"Well, that's what I wanted at first. Before I found out what play it was."

"Well, heavens, girl—then you succeeded! You met your goal admirably. You're in the play, and you've got a very important role."

"What?"

"Why, you're the Fairy Godmother, didn't you hear?"

"No, I guess I—"

"And she's where all the magic is. She's the one who makes it all happen. And do you want to know why we chose you for that role? Because she has to change from an old woman to a beautiful young fairy. She's two different people, almost. And you're a good actress. You can pull that off."

"You really think so?"

"Oh, I'm sure you can!"

"My mother was hoping I would play Cinderella. She has a lace tablecloth."

Mrs. McLean looked puzzled for a moment but then grinned. "Your mother's a big girl. She can get over it if you can."

"Okay," Dorothy felt somehow as if a weight had been lifted off her back. "I guess I'm ready now."

"Good." Mrs. McLean got up and offered Dorothy her hand. "Let's go back, then. Don't forget your backpack. And oh, Dorothy," she added as they walked down the hall together toward the activity room and the first *Cinderella* rehearsal, "wait'll you see what we've got lined up for your magical transformation!"

Where in the World Did All These Bananas Come From?

BY RON FRIDELL

If we gave out awards for the World's Most Successful Fruit, which kind do you think would win first prize? Apples? Oranges? Peaches? Cherries? Nope. The grand prize winner would have to be bananas, no question about it.

What makes bananas the all-time number one king of fruit? For one thing, there are so many of them all around the world. Bananas, bananas, everywhere! Guess which fruit people eat more of than any other. That's right: bananas. On six continents—North America, South America, Europe, Africa, Asia, and Australia—the banana reigns supreme.

And bananas are so handy to eat. Each one comes in its own cheerful, bright yellow wrapper. You just peel away the peel and there you have it: a delicious, nutritious treat.

Nutritious? That's right, bananas are as good for your health as they are tasty. They're just chock-full of carbohydrates. Those are the energy-rich sugars and starches that help you to run faster and jump higher. Athletes especially love bananas because they are such an abundant energy source.

Bananas are terrific brain food too. As you sit there thinking all those clever thoughts and getting all those bright ideas, your brain is hard at work, fueled by sugary stuff called glucose, and bananas are rich in glucose.

Bananas are so fine in so many ways. The word *bananas* is even fun to spell. All together now: "B-A-N-A-N-A-S." It sounds like you keep starting all over again and you'll never finish, doesn't it?

Speaking of words, have you ever looked at those little stickers stuck to most banana peels in the store? Peel one off sometime and take a look. The sticker often names the place where the banana was grown.

Are bananas grown in the United States? Yes, mostly in Hawaii and California. But there are nowhere near enough bananas grown in the United States to supply all the bananas that people eat. Each year the average American eats 28 pounds of bananas. How many bananas do you think you eat in a week? How many in a year?

So where do all those bananas in stores all across the United States come from? A lot of them come from Ecuador, Colombia, and other South American nations that are thousands of miles away. These faraway places grow tons and tons of bananas. Some are grown on small farms, some on huge plantations.

And which country buys the most bananas from these nations? If you guessed the United States, you were right. Every year the United States imports more than 8 *billion* pounds of bananas.

Imports? When one country buys a product from another country, it's called *importing*. The United States *imports* bananas from other countries. The opposite of *import* is *export*. Those other countries *export*, or *send*, bananas to the United States in exchange for money. *Import*: buy from another country. *Export*: sell to another country.

How do exported bananas get from those distant plantations all the way to the United States? Let's follow the bananas that begin on a banana plantation in Ecuador. Bananas are one of Ecuador's most valuable resources, second only to the oil they have underground. Ecuador is a tropical country that borders the Pacific Ocean. It's warm and wet the whole year round, and that's the kind of weather that banana plants just love.

Field workers plant banana plants in long, straight rows with ditches in between for drainage. When banana plants grow up, they look a lot like trees. Some grow to be as tall as a two-story house, with lots of big green leaves. And what about the bananas themselves? Well, there are some surprises. For one thing, they grow in a surprising direction. You'd expect bananas to hang downward from the stem, like apples or oranges, wouldn't you? But the stem is at the bottom and the bananas grow upward from it in thick, tall, curving bunches.

And something else is surprising about bananas: While they're still growing on the trees, field workers wrap each bunch in a clear plastic bag. That's right—big bunches of bananas growing inside plastic bags. The bags help shut out insects and keep the fruit from getting all blemished and spotted.

The field workers also prune the plants. They cut away some of the leaves to make sure the bananas get plenty of nourishing sunlight. There is something surprising about the shiny green banana leaves too. They are so flexible and waterproof that workers sometimes wear these leaves on their heads as sunshades and umbrellas.

Field workers must keep the plants free of pests as well. Yes, bananas have enemies. Mice and rats, for instance, like to climb the plant and eat the bananas while they're still growing.

And pesky gophers love to chomp away at the plant from down below. Sometimes they eat so much of the base that the whole plant topples over—KA-BOOM!

When harvest time arrives, field workers with big curved knives called machetes sever the bunches of bananas from the trees. The shirts the workers wear have padded shoulders. Why? After cutting the tall bunches of bananas, they carry each bunch gently on their softly padded shoulders so as not to bruise the fruit.

Next, the bunches go to packing sheds, where they are placed into tanks of water and washed. Then they are packed in cartons lined with plastic padding, also to guard against bruising.

When the bananas are harvested, they are still hard and green. They will start to ripen and turn yellow in a couple of weeks. Before then, they must complete a journey of thousands of miles by sea, from Ecuador to their U.S. destination.

The next step is to quickly transport them from the plantation to an ocean-going banana ship that waits at the ocean port city of Guayquil. Some plantations are located in remote areas near a river, so to get to the ocean, the bananas are carried out by large hovercraft, amphibious vehicles that move low along the riverbed on a curtain of air created by jet engines. But most of the plantations send their bananas out by truck or train—unless there is an emergency.

Tropical countries like Ecuador have lots of rain, which sometimes leads to flooding that is so severe that the plantation becomes isolated. Nothing on the ground can get in or get out.

What then? The bananas can't wait. If they don't get going on their journey right away, they'll ripen before they reach their destination. So emergency helicopters fly in and lower long ropes with slings to carry the bunches away, just like they rescue people trapped in floods.

At the ocean port in Guayquil, the packed bananas are loaded into metal containers and the containers are loaded into hatches, or big topside doors, on refrigerated banana ships. They will be kept at temperatures around 58 degrees for the next seven days, while the ship sails eastward and northward through the Panama Canal and up the East Coast of the United States.

Bananas are delivered to U.S. ports all over the nation. This particular banana ship is bound for New York City. Once it arrives on shore, dock workers carefully unload the contents. Then forklift trucks haul the cartons of bananas into a warehouse that is bigger than a football field.

From there, trucks come to pick up their orders and deliver them to supermarkets and small neighborhood stores in New York and other cities in the Northeastern United States. Hopefully, the bananas will arrive firm and undamaged. Have you noticed how careful everyone has been in handling the bananas all along the way, from plantation to warehouse? You probably can imagine why. Bananas bruise easily, and the more perfect they look, the more people will want to buy them.

By the time the bananas arrive at the store, they should be getting close to ripe. The peels should still be at least partly green, which means the fruit inside is getting sweet and ready for eating. Now the bananas, imported all the way from Ecuador, are ready to be purchased and brought home.

Some people like to buy bananas while they're still green. That way they don't have to eat them right away. They can leave them a few days to ripen at home. If you plan to eat a banana the same day, though, you should buy one that's totally yellow with a stem that is just slightly green. That way it's at its peak of freshness and will be most delicious to eat.

Sometimes, though, people deliberately let bananas get overripe and turn soft. They wait until the peel gets full of those familiar brown speckles called "sugar spots." Remember, bananas contain lots of glucose and other kinds of sugar. When the sugar spots show up, the banana's sugar content is at its peak, and that means the banana has turned sweet and soft, which makes it perfect for mashing and blending.

Which brings us to the delicious subject of banana recipes. On a hot day, how about a banana smoothie made with yogurt, cold milk, and a banana, all whooshed together in a blender. You'll want a nice soft banana for that. Or how about banana bread, or banana muffins, banana pancakes, banana fritters, banana yogurt, or banana bread pudding? Or how about a nice grilled peanut butter and banana sandwich. You probably would prefer a firm banana for that.

Well, this brings us to the end of our journey from a banana plantation in Ecuador to the supermarket or neighborhood grocery store. The next time you stop in, go where the bananas are and take a look at a sticker to see which nation they were imported from. And think of all the people and trucks and ships and gentle care it took to deliver this all-time number one king of fruit from those faraway tropical fields to you.

A Trip to Mega Mart

"Now, I'll just click print and my report will be finished," Laura said. She clicked, but nothing happened. The printer just sat there, silent.

"No paper! Arghhh," Laura sighed. "Mom, the printer is out of paper. I have to turn my report in tomorrow and the printer is out of paper."

"Calm down, Laura," her mom called back. "I'm going to Mega Mart this evening. I'll add computer paper to the list of things we need."

"You're going to Mega Mart!" Laura exclaimed. "My report is finished, and I cleaned my room. Can I go with you?" Laura pleaded.

"Yes, Laura, you may go with me. Go ask your dad if there is anything he needs to add to the shopping list."

Laura found her dad in the garage washing the car. "Dad, Mom and I are going to Mega Mart after dinner. Do you need anything?"

"No, thanks. I'm good," said Laura's dad. "Wait, Laura. You know what? I could use a new hose. Someone left this one out in the yard and I ran over it with the lawnmower. Now it's sprung a leak."

"Uh, yeah, sorry about that," Laura apologized. "Mega Mart has a lawn and garden section. Why don't you come with us?"

"Sounds like a plan," said her dad.

After dinner, Laura helped her mom with the dishes. Then they all piled into the family van. Laura could hardly wait to get to Mega Mart. It was her favorite store. It was bright and clean and had everything a ten-year-old girl could want.

"Okay," said Laura's mom as she grabbed a cart. "We don't have a lot of time before the store closes, so why don't we split up."

"I can show Dad where the garden center is," said Laura.

"Great. You guys pick up a new garden hose and some computer paper, while I do the grocery shopping. I'll meet you at the front of the store in twenty minutes."

"Lead the way," Laura's dad said to her.

Laura picked up a shopping basket and headed off in the direction of the garden center with her dad trailing behind her.

"Slow down, Laura," her dad called. "Look at this. They have tennis shoes here, and they're on sale. What a bargain!"

"I told you they have just about everything," Laura explained.

"I've been meaning to pick up a new pair of tennis shoes. The ones I have now squeak every time a take a step."

"Dad, we're supposed to be picking out a garden hose," said Laura. "I guess you could use a new pair of shoes, though. The squeak, squeak, squeak *is* really annoying."

Laura's dad chose a pair of shoes and placed them in the shopping basket. "To the garden center," he directed.

"Yes, to the garden center," Laura agreed. "Can we stop in the girls section on the way?" she asked. "I just remembered that I need new gym socks. My favorite pair have a hole in the toe."

"Okay," her dad replied, "but we need to watch the time. We only have fifteen minutes until we have to meet your mom."

"I know just what I want. It'll take two seconds."

Laura led her dad through racks of brightly colored clothing. She grabbed a package of tube socks and tossed them in her basket. Another pack of socks, white ones with little pastel pom-poms attached to the ankles, caught her eye. Laura hastily tossed those in the basket too.

"Find what you need?" her dad called from the end of the aisle.

"Got 'em," said Laura. "Now, let's get that garden hose."

Laura led her dad to the back of the store where the garden center was located. "Dad, here's a hose just like the old one," Laura said as she pointed to the top shelf.

"Excellent!" said her dad as he pulled a hose down and placed it in their basket. "Since we're here," he added, "I'm going to look for a new spray nozzle."

Laura stood at the end of the aisle looking at a display of seed packets while her father browsed the garden tools. After only a few minutes he came back and added a nozzle, a pair of gardening gloves, and new pruning sheers to the basket.

"Dad, maybe we should get a cart," complained Laura. "This shopping basket is getting heavy."

"We're almost finished, Kiddo," her dad said. "I can carry the basket."

Laura's dad took the basket and shifted its contents to even out the weight. It was indeed heavy, he thought. "Okay, what else do we need to get?" he asked.

"I think we've got everything," Laura said. "Besides, our time is up. Mom is probably already waiting for us up front."

"Are you sure we got everything?" Laura's dad asked. "I thought there was something you needed for school."

"Oh, computer paper!" exclaimed Laura. "I can't believe I almost forgot. I need computer paper so I can print out my report that is due tomorrow."

Again, Laura maneuvered through the aisles while her dad struggled to keep up with her. Locating the aisle of office supplies was easy for Laura, but deciding which paper to buy was not. She found the plain white computer paper, which was what she needed for her report, but she also found a variety of colored papers and specialty papers.

"Dad," Laura said, "I need white paper for my report, but I want some of this paper with the polka-dotted border too. It's the perfect paper for writing to my pen pal."

Laura's dad motioned to her with the overflowing shopping basket. "Just put what you want in the basket so we can get going," he said. "We're supposed to meet your mom, and we're late!"

Laura tossed both types of paper into the basket and then turned toward the front of the store. As she and her father rounded the corner of the front aisle, Laura could see her mom standing there, impatiently tapping her fingertips on the handle of her shopping cart. "Where have the two of you been?" she asked as they approached her. "The store is going to close in fifteen minutes."

Both Laura and her dad grinned. "We found a few other things we needed," they replied in unison.

"I see that," said Laura's mother as she glanced at their shopping basket. "Things you *needed* or things you *wanted*?" she asked.

"A few of each, I guess," said Laura's dad.

"Well, I can see that both of you need a lesson about responsible shopping," Laura's mom scolded. "Do you see this list?" she asked as she held up a piece of paper. "I made this list before we left for the store, keeping in mind what we need and how much money we have to spend. Shopping with a list helps me stick to the family budget. Laura, you know what a budget is, don't you? Didn't you have a homework assignment about budgets not too long ago?"

"Mr. G. taught us about budgets," Laura replied. She looked at her dad as she continued, "Budgets are tools that help you plan how much of your money you want to save and how much of your money you want to spend."

"That's right," said Laura's mom. "And since we want to take a special family vacation next summer, it's important that we stick to our budget. Let's compare what you have in your basket with what's on the shopping list. Are there things in there you don't really need?"

"Well, I need the computer paper for my report," explained Laura.

"And that's on our list," said Laura's mom.

"I guess I don't really need the fancy paper, though. I can print my pen pal letters on regular paper and then draw my own decorations."

"Good idea, Laura," her mom said proudly. "Go ahead and put the computer paper in the cart. Now what about you?" she continued as she turned to look at Laura's dad.

"Well, I definitely need a new garden hose so I can water the roses. I can get along just fine with my old gardening gloves and pruning sheers, though."

"Okay," said Laura's mom, "the hose goes in the cart, but the other gardening items do not."

Laura peered into the basket to see what was left. "I know gym socks are not on our shopping list," she explained. "But all of my socks worn thin. Can I get the tube socks as long as I put the package of fancy socks back?"

"That seems like a fair compromise," said Laura's mom.

"Well, that just leaves my tennis shoes." Laura's dad said. "My old shoes are perfectly fine; it's just that the squeak is *so* annoying."

Laura and her mom looked at each other and giggled. "It is annoying!" they cried. "Put the shoes in the cart!"

"Okay, we're done shopping then, right?" Laura said.

"Right," her mom agreed. "Why don't you and your dad put the items left in the basket back on the shelves, while I get in line," she suggested.

Laura took the basket and led her dad back through the maze of aisles. They returned the polka-dotted paper, the fancy socks, the gardening gloves, and the pruning sheers to their proper places and rejoined Laura's mom just as she was getting ready to check out.

As Laura peeked into the shopping cart to see if she could guess what her mom would pack in her lunch this week, she noticed a bag of chips. She glanced at the shopping list sticking out of her mom's purse. Chips weren't on the list. "Mom," Laura asked, "do you *want* those potato chips, or do you *need* those potato chips?"

"All right, Laura, you caught me!" exclaimed her mom. "You and your father can put those back too!"

Where Do You Keep Your Money?

By Gail Karlitz

Let's agree on one thing right from the start. If you want to make your money grow, the worst place to keep it is in the pocket of your jeans. You know what happens . . . you either spend it right away or forget to take it out of your pocket. Eventually, your jeans end up on the floor, right there with the rest of the clothes you've worn all week, your schoolbooks, the blanket you kicked off your bed, and other assorted treasures.

But what about keeping your money in your room—in a safe place, like a piggy bank?

There are a lot of good reasons to keep your money safe in your room. For one thing, it's right there when you need it. You can get to it quickly and easily. Another good thing is that you always know exactly how much money you have. You can take it out any time and count it.

Of course, the very reason why keeping your money in your room is good can also be the reason why keeping your money in your room is bad. Let's suppose you are saving your money for something big, like a new bike. Your savings are growing nicely. You know that you shouldn't touch your bike money. But there it is, right in your room, in that piggy bank.

It's calling to you. "Come and get me. You know you want to spend me." Money in a piggy bank is money that is easy to spend.

Another thing about keeping your money in a piggy bank is that the amount of money you have is never more that what you have put into the piggy bank. If you put in $5 every month, after a year you will have $60. After ten years, you will have $600. No more, no less.

Money Word:

INFLATION: the general increase in the cost of everything, from cars and houses to burgers and fries.

That means in ten years, $600 won't buy nearly as much stuff as it will now.

Think about what has happened to the buying power of money. In 1960, a kid with a quarter could buy a slice of pizza for 15¢ and a soda for 10¢. Today, you'd probably need at least $2 to buy the same meal! In 1960, a kid who had saved $7 could buy a really great pair of sneakers. Today, you could use that $7 to buy some very cool sneaker laces.

Many adults love to talk about the good old days and how low prices were back then. They sometimes forget that incomes were pretty low then too. In 1960, the average income per person in this country was $2,219 per year! By 2000, the average income per person was $29,676.

Aside from the fact that a specific amount of money loses some of its buying power as time goes by, there's one more reason why people usually don't keep their money at home.

If you have a lot of money (which would be a really nice problem to have), it gets a little hard to find places for it all.

Of course, no one would really keep a million dollar bills around. They would at least trade them in for ten thousand hundred-dollar bills!

Our government does print money in higher denominations than hundred-dollar bills, but those bills are not used by the general public.

It just doesn't make sense to keep your money at home. You're tempted to spend it, and the prices of the things you want keep going up. The longer you hold on to your money, the less it's worth. And, if you did save a fortune, you'd break your back trying to lift it all!

Wait! Don't rush out and spend all your money right now!

There are many ways you can save your money so that the amount you put in actually grows, even if you don't add a cent more. When you do that, you are making your money earn more money for you. You are an investor.

Zach: The Yard-Sale Whiz

Zach Bissonnette, 11, jumped out of bed before 7 A.M. After gulping down orange juice and a granola bar, he and his mom head out for Saturday morning yard sales near his Cape Cod, Mass., home.

Zach didn't spend any money at the first five yard sales. But at the sixth he hit pay dirt: a console game system with two games for $7! Each component was still wrapped in plastic in the Styrofoam tray compartments. Although played with, the system had been so carefully repackaged it was what dealers call "mint-in-box."

"Would you take $5?" Zach asked. The seller agreed, and Zach paid with his allowance. He still had $10 left.

Money doesn't burn a hole in Zach's pocket. He's a patient and careful shopper, and knows how to get value for his dollar. He buys at yard sales, flea markets, rummage sales, and thrift shops whenever he can. "It's the best way to recycle," he says. "It's good for the environment, and fun. It's going hunting."

Zach, a sixth-grade student, even snares clothes bargains! Last spring he wore khaki slacks, a shirt and tie, navy blazer and loafers to an interview at Cape Cod Academy. Everything had been purchased either at yard sales or rummage sales!

MORE FUN THAN THE MALL

"While driving home from yard sales I add up the retail (store) price on books I bought. Then I compare them to the prices I actually paid—usually 25 cents for paperbacks and 50 cents or $1 for hardcover books," Zach says. "On a typical day I might get two or three Matt Christopher books, a Gary Paulsen and maybe a couple of Beverly Cleary or Hardy Boys books, all in excellent condition. Retail price might come to $25, but I'd have spent $2.50."

"Once you see what great things you can buy this way and how much fun it is, malls seem dull. One of my favorite finds last summer was a collapsible aluminum golf card that was just about new. [Zach plays tennis and golf.] We paid $5 for it and saw the same cart for $80 at a discount golf store the next week. Last week we bought a basket for a friend's new kitties to sleep in. We bought our aquarium complete with stand for $10 last year. My mom loves that my new jacket cost $5 instead of $70!"

Zach mainly buys sports equipment, games, magazines and books, and adds to his collection of old video games and systems. But he also keeps his eye out for "smalls"—collectibles such as the figurine that he bought for a quarter. He can resell these at a profit, either at his favorite Internet auction site, or at a local consignment shop.

At his sixth yard sale of the day, Zach scores again. He finds a set of skis that were used only a few times and then outgrown. When the man selling them reduces the $40 price by half, Zach's mom buys the skis and poles for him. At $20, they cost about the same as renting skis for a weekend! And when Zach outgrows them, they can probably be resold.

At the last yard sales of the day, Zach buys a backpack with matching notebook, unused (with tags attached), for $1!

ZACH'S TIPS FOR SHOPPING YARD SALES

1. Resist temptation to overspend. Don't buy what you don't really want or need, just because the price is low.
2. Inspect your selections carefully. Look for chips, stains, wear, and tear.
3. Prices are rarely firm. You can make a fair offer, or just politely ask, "Can you do any better?" You can frequently get 25 percent off the asking price.
4. Be very careful when buying anything electric or electronic. Make sure it works. Ask a parent for advice.
5. Know the retail (store) prices of things you want to buy. Expect to pay about one-quarter of the retail price when you buy at a yard sale.
6. Keep your eye out for gifts. Does your mom or dad like to cook? Does your little brother or sister collect action figures?
7. Party and holiday clothes are usually a good buy. Kids often wear these clothes only once or twice before outgrowing them!
8. Clean what you buy. Can it be washed or dry-cleaned? Ask for advice.
9. The early bird gets the best picks—but prices often drop in the afternoon.
10. Be proud of what you buy this way. Tell people if you want to—consider it a sign of being a smart consumer!

Swamp Scramblers

BY DIANE THUNA

Running across shoreline sludge, sometimes leaping high into the air, the mudskipper is a fish out of water. But it's definitely not out of place. Though they're truly fish—with fins and gills to prove it—mudskippers are so at home on land, they can not only walk and breathe air, they can also climb trees.

Sound weird? Maybe, but then the world they live in—the mangrove swamps and mud flats of Asia, Africa, and the South Pacific—is a pretty unusual one as well. Covered with water at high tide and a lot of oozing muck when the water goes back down, these areas can seem inhospitable. Yet mangrove trees flourish here. Propped up by their long, stilt-like roots, these trees are able to both rise above the waves and stand firm in the shifting mud. They also provide the climbing mudskippers with the perfect place to snatch a meal of insects or spiders and a safe refuge at high tide, when larger predatory fish patrol the water below.

How do mudskippers move on land? The answer lies in their fins. The sturdy fins near the front of the fish are not only extremely strong, they're also bent to look a lot like arms. Supporting its weight on these fins, the mudskipper lifts its body off the ground and pushes itself forward at the same time, a bit like a seal. The fins at the back of its body are the ones the mudskipper uses when climbing. Shaped like small suckers, they allow the fish to cling to mangrove roots while their front fins find a good grip even farther up the limb. When frightened, the mudskipper can also scurry across the mud or leap into the air with a few powerful lashes from its tail.

Of course, being able to move on land is no good if you can't also breathe. Mudskippers have that problem licked too. Amazingly, they have been known to survive out of water for two and a half days. Most other fish would die in just a fraction of that time. That's because all fish, even mudskippers, use their gills to get oxygen from water. The gills are packed with tiny blood vessels, and, as the water passes over them, the oxygen in the water is absorbed into the fish's bloodstream. Normally when fish leave the water, their gills dry out and become useless. Not a mudskipper's gills, though—they're always moist!

Before leaving the water, mudskippers soak up water into special gill chambers, which are storage pockets located around each gill. Once on land, the fish can absorb oxygen from this stored water by rolling its large, movable eyes back into its eye sockets. This movement swirls the stored water around the pouch and remoistens the gills. It's a great trick, but there's one small catch: eating. As mudskippers swallow insects and other tasty treats, the water stored in the gill chambers floods out, leaving the mudskipper high and dry. Then the fish has to quickly scoot back to a nearby puddle for a refill.

But moist gills are only part of the answer for the land-loving mudskipper. Mudskippers can also soak up oxygen through their skin, as long as it is kept wet. Some scientists think that's why mudskippers role in mud puddles or lounge on the sun-drenched flats with their tails in the water.

The Trap-Door Spider's Secret Hideaway

BY MARNE VENTURA

Have you ever had a secret hiding place? Maybe you've made a tent by hanging a blanket between two chairs and crept inside to read or think. Maybe you've even put up a sign that said "Keep Out!" so your family would know you wanted to be alone for a while If you like secret hiding places, you'll love the trap-door spider's home. It's so well camouflaged that even if you were sitting on the ground nearby, you probably wouldn't see it.

If you know how to look, however, trap-door spiders can be found in warm climates around the world. In the southwestern United States, these brownish spiders are about the size of a quarter—but in southeastern Asia, they can grow to four inches!

To build its home, a trap-door spider digs a hole in the ground about eight inches deep and an inch wide. The spider uses mouthparts called chelicerae that have teeth like a comb to scoop up dirt. Then the spider forms the dirt into a ball and tosses it out of the hole with its strong hind legs.

The trap-door spider works hard to make its house just right. When the burrow is big enough, the spider coats the sides with a mixture of soil and saliva to make them smooth, hard, and waterproof.

Then it spins sheets of silk to cover the walls. Spider silk makes amazing wallpaper: a thread of silk is stronger than a thread of steel the same thickness. In the trap-door spider's home, this layer of silk reinforces the burrow walls and makes it easier for the spider to move around.

To camouflage the burrow, the spider makes a door of silk and dirt and places it on top of the hole like a tightly fitting lid. The sticky silk holds the dirt together, making the door strong and solid. The spider bevels the edges with its fangs and spins a tough silk hinge so the door can open and close. The spider even uses silk to glue twigs, leaves, and moss on top, so the door looks just like the ground around it.

By building such a clever home, the trap-door spider solves three big problems: how to find food, how to protect itself, and how to raise its young.

During the night, the spider hunts. It sits underneath its burrow lid until it feels the vibration of an insect on the ground above. Using its hind legs to anchor itself inside the burrow, the spider throws open the door with its front legs, grabs the passing insect, pulls it inside, and shuts the door—all in less than a second!

The burrow's strong lid protects the spider from animals looking for an eight-legged snack. The spider simply stays inside with the door shut, and most passing predators—birds, lizards, frogs and toads, other spiders, and some insects—don't know it's there.

If a predator tries to open the door to attack, the spider uses its fangs and front legs to hold the door shut while it braces its back legs against the sides of the burrow.

Wasps are a trap-door spider's worst enemy because they can dig through the door with their sharp jaws. Some trap-door spiders outsmart wasps by building secret rooms for hiding or side tunnels with emergency exits. Or they simply keep the burrow entrance blocked with a solid earthen plug up to an inch thick.

The trap-door spider's home provides a safe place for the female to raise her young. The silk lining helps keep the burrow warm and dry in winter and cool and dry in summer. A female trap-door spider lays her eggs—as many as two hundred—at the bottom of the burrow. She stays with the eggs until they hatch, and then guards and feeds the spiderlings until they are old enough to go out and dig their own burrows nearby.

Trap-door spiders are very shy and are not dangerous to humans. When they're full-grown, male trap-door spiders leave their homes to find a mate. Aside from that (and when they pop out to grab their dinner at night!) trap-door spiders like to stay hidden inside their burrows. Female trap-door spiders tend to live longer than males, with some females living over twenty years without ever leaving home!

Maybe someday you'll be lucky enough to see a trap-door spider's home. When you do, take a good look— but don't disturb the spider hiding inside. If it could make a sign like you can, the sign would say "Keep Out!"

Tree House Trouble

BY SALLY DERBY MILLER

Sam was stubborn and liked to do things his own way. He liked to eat his meals one food at a time—no mixing. At bat, he like to dig his foot into the dust, swing the bat three times, then settle it on his shoulder. He always swung at the second pitch. He wore his purple socks on Tuesdays and his lucky sweater whenever he had a spelling test.

Oscar was Sam's father. He liked to do things his own way, too. While the neighbors mowed their lawns, Oscar grew a wildflower meadow. He got a haircut on the first Thursday of every month, whether he needed it or not. And he wore his lucky sweater to every one of Sam's ball games.

Sam thought his dad was the smartest man on earth, and his dad thought Sam was the finest son a man could ever want . . . until the day they decided to build the tree house.

Sam had a picture in his mind.

Oscar had a picture in his mind.

The pictures didn't match.

At the lumberyard and the hardware store, they disagreed on how much wood to buy. They bickered about how long the nails should be. They quarreled about what color paint they should pick. And when they got home, they argued and ARGUED and ARGUED about which tree was best.

Sam wanted the maple. He wouldn't give in.

His dad wanted the hackberry. He wouldn't give in, either.

The boards and nails and the paint sat in the backyard.

They sat there in the hot, summer sunshine. They sat there when the autumn leaves fell. They sat under a blanket of snow all winter.

"Sam is so stubborn," Sam's dad complained to Sam's mother. "If he'd listen to reason, I could show him why the hackberry is best."

"Why won't Dad listen to my ideas?" Sam asked his mom. "He wants to do everything his way."

Sam's mother tried talking to Sam's dad. He wouldn't listen. She tried talking to Sam. It did no good.

Sam stayed stubborn, and Oscar stayed obstinate.

Spring came. The wildflower meadow began to bloom, and baseball practice started. Soon it was Mother's Day, and Sam made his mother a clay pot and filled it with flowers. She loved it.

Now Father's Day was coming up. Sam thought and thought and finally decided on a present for his dad. He would take some of the lumber they'd bought for the tree and build his dad a fancy box for keys and change.

Sam sawed and pounded while his mom supervised. The saw kept sticking and the nails were too long. It was a dumb box, Sam decided. He would throw it in the trash.

Just then his dad wandered out into the backyard. "Hey, did you make that box for me?" he asked Sam.

"It was going to be for Father's Day," Sam said, "but I couldn't do a very good job. I'll buy you something instead."

"Oh no! I like this," said his dad. "It's just what I need to keep my keys in." Then he added, "Your mother says if we're not going to make a tree house, we should move this pile of lumber into the garage. Will you help?"

"Sure," said Sam. He picked up a board with a big knothole in it. "I was going to use this one for the back door," he said sadly. "The knothole would have made a great peephole."

Sam's dad looked at him in surprise. "You planned on a back door?" he asked

Sam nodded. "And a porch."

"I was thinking of towers," his dad told him. "Like a castle might have."

Sam looked at him. "Castles can have back doors."

His dad nodded. "And a drawbridge is like a front porch."

"But we still don't which tree is best," Sam said.

Sam looked at the maple.

His dad looked at the hackberry tree.

Sam's mother looked out the window. "Well, my dear obstinate Oscar and stubborn Sam, if you're going to make a tree house after all," she said, "why not put it in the oak?"

Sam and his dad grinned at each other.

"Magnificent Mom has spoken," Sam said. "What do you think?"

"I think it's a great idea," said Sam's dad. "Let's get to work!"

Read About Cesar Chavez

BY Stephen Feinstein

Cesar Chavez was born in Arizona on March 31, 1927. He grew up on his family's farm.

Cesar's grandfather was a poor farmer in Mexico. He came north looking for a better life in the United States.

Cesar's grandfather bought a farm. He grew crops on the farm. The Chavez family paid workers to help them pick the crops. The farm workers moved from job to job. They were called migrant farm workers.

In 1937, Cesar was ten years old. It did not rain much that year. Crops did not grow. Cesar's father could not pay his bills. So the Chavez family lost their farm. They had nothing but an old car. Farm work was the only work they could do.

In the fall, the Chavez family became migrant farm workers too. They picked vegetables and fruits. They moved from farm to farm in California. Sometimes they had to sleep in their car. Sometimes they stayed in work camps. The camps were not clean.

Life was very hard. Even the children had to work picking fruit or vegetables. Workers got paid for each box they filled. It took a long time to fill a box with fruit. They made only a few cents a day. The farm owners did not care.

Cesar wanted to help migrant farm workers. But he did not know what to do. Other workers came together in unions to fight for their rights. But farm workers could not do this.

In 1945, Cesar went into the Navy. He got out in 1948. Then he went back to work in the fields.

In 1952, Cesar met Fred Ross. Ross worked for the Community Service Organization, or CSO. Cesar helped Ross to get the workers together. Ross showed the workers how to vote. He showed them how to fight for their rights. In 1958 Cesar became head of the CSO.

In 1962, Cesar started a union for migrant workers. Then he got a great idea. He asked people not to buy any grapes until the workers made more money. Many people stopped buying grapes. The farm owners gave in.

Later, Cesar started a new union. Cesar's union got California to pass a new work law. Migrant farm workers now have the same rights as other workers.

Cesar Chavez died on April 23, 1993. His hard work made life better for migrant farm workers.

The Organizer

BY J. PATRICK LEWIS

Cesar Chavez
Migrant Labor Organizer (1927—1993)

Cesar was a peaceable fighter
With his back against the wall.
He was the David to Goliaths,
One worker against them all.

Up from the Mexican culture,
He rallied migrants to unite
And challenged consumers to boycott
Five years for the grape pickers' plight.

Cesar won and lost many battles
But never resorted to arms,
And carried the torch for *La Causa*
Across California farms.

Poor migrants, whose harvest was hunger,
Depended on him to be strong,
To ignite the fight and fight for right
And everywhere right the wrong.

The Rampanion

Alison DeSmyter knows about the problems people have in wheelchairs. Alison was born with cerebral palsy, a condition that makes it difficult to control muscles. So Alison has used a wheelchair most of her life.

One common problem for wheelchair users is crossing streets with curbs. To get her chair over a curb, Alison needed somebody to push or lift her chair. She wanted more independence. So Alison invented the Rampanion—a portable ramp that allows a wheelchair to move easily over a curb.

Alison first thought of the Rampanion when she was asked to do an invention project for school she had just two weeks. That wasn't much time to design something as complicated as the Rampanion.

But Alison did it.

First Alison thought about making a rubber ramp, but she decided it would be too bulky to carry around. Next she considered an inflatable ramp. That wouldn't do, either—it would always need to be blown up. Finally Alison decided to make a ramp out of lightweight metal. This type of ramp could be easily folded and carried.

Alison began by building a small model of her ramp from Popsicle sticks. Once she had built the model, she thought about the type of metal she'd use for the real thing.

The Rampanion needed to be light yet strong, so Alison decided on aluminum. Her father found some aluminum where he works, and he helped Alison put the ramp together. To build the ramp, they needed a lot of exact measurements, which Alison took herself.

As Alison and her father built the Rampanion, they thought of improvements they could make to its design. They added an edge to the Rampanion's sides, to keep a chair's wheels on track. They put sticky tape on the bottom, to help secure the Rampanion to any surface—even in the rain.

The completed Rampanion weighs only four pounds. When it's folded, it can be carried in its own cloth bag. The bag can be attached to a wheelchair.

Alison's Rampanion won the fifth-grade grand prize for the third annual Houston Inventor's Showcase Exposition. Her prize was a trip to Florida. The trip included visits to Disneyworld, the Kennedy Space Center, and Thomas Edison's estate. Thomas Edison was a great inventor who created many electrical devices, such as the light bulb and the phonograph.

Alison hasn't stopped inventing things for wheelchair users. She's working on a Handy Helper, which is a tray that attaches to a wheelchair. The Handy Helper allows people in wheelchairs to be served more easily in cafeterias and fast-food restaurants.

Mrs. McBloom, Clean Up Your Classroom!

BY KELLY DIPUCCHIO

It's a fact that nearly every school from Kennebunkport, Maine to Chickaloon, Alaska, has one teacher whose classroom is a sorry, jumbled-up mess. Knickerbocker Elementary in the pint-size town of Up Yonder was no exception.

Mrs. McBloom in Room Five had a classroom that would impress even the most clutter-lovin' junkyard dog. It was a heap of mess on account of her never cleaning it—not *once* in fifty years of teaching!

Every year, Mrs. McBloom's students yammered, "Mrs. McBloom, clean up your classroom!"

For decades, Principal Pumpernickel pleaded, "Mrs. McBloom, clean up your classroom!"

Twenty-two janitors came and went over the years. They *all* grumbled, "Mrs. McBloom, clean up your classroom!"

"Oh, higgly-piggly," Mrs. McBloom would say. "It's on my to-do list." Truth is, it had been on her to-do list for nearly forty-five years. "See, it's listed right here above *Take a fancy-shmancy cruise.*"

Now one week before Mrs. McBloom was fixin' to retire, her room looked like this: giant sunflowers dropped over desks like decorative lamps; tangly vines with fat green beans climbed the walls; and a genuine, full-grown Ruby Red apple tree grew smack-dab in the middle of her classroom.

Years of science experiments had left all kinds of critters hoppin' and cluckin' and flyin' around Room Five. Chickens laid eggs in the coat cubbies. Butterflies fluttered back and forth between children's heads and pencil erasers.

Now something drastic had to be done right quick. Sweet young Miss Bumblesprout was preparing to take Mrs. McBloom's place in the fall. Miss Bumblesprout fretted, "Mrs. McBloom, clean up your room! Pretty please?"

"Oh, higgly-piggly," sighed Mrs. McBloom, scratching her beehive hairdo. "I've backed myself into a pickle. How am I *ever* going to get this room cleaned up in a jiffy?"

The rooster perched on the piano belted out a hearty *cock-a-doodle-dooo!*

"That a *humdinger* of an idea, Rudy! Much obliged," said Mrs. McBloom. Mrs. McBloom moved a cluster of frogs aside and wrote an assignment on the board.

Homework: Come up with an idea to get Room #5 tidy. Lickety split. Be Creative! STRETCH your imagination; use your *Noggin!* Anything goes!!!!

By the end of the following week, the whole class was bustin' with excitement. One by one, kids came to the front of the room (just past the mushroom patch, but before the mountain of unclaimed mittens and gym sneakers) to share ideas.

Sam Wigglesworth had invented a Super-Duper-Picker-Upper-Thingamabob. "It can pick up from zero to ten in sixty seconds!"

Lilly Lumpkin suggest Mrs. McBloom hire a magician. "Then abracadabra! Everything will disappear!"

Cooper Butterbaker brought a heard of hungry goats from his daddy's farm to demonstrate their voracious appetites. "They once ate a rusty pickup truck in three hours flat!"

On and on the ideas kept coming. Mrs. McBloom recorded them on the chalkboard. Georgia Peachpit was the last student to raise her hand. She stepped over the world globe, shooed Cooper's goats, and unrolled a colorful poster board.

Help Mrs. McBloom Clean Up Her Room Day! All of Up Yonder is invited Saturday 10:00 a.m. If each citizen shows up to remove ONE item, Room 5 will be tidy lickety-split. Free eggs and apples to everyone who helps.

"By Georgia, that's it!" hollered Mrs. McBloom. "A dilly of an idea!"

Word of "Help Mrs. McBloom Clean Up her Room Day" spread through the town faster than Corky Redman's chicken pox in the spring of '99.

Seeing as nearly every citizen of Up Yonder had been a student of Mrs. McBloom's at one time or another, the whole town showed up on Saturday to help. A line loop-de-looped through the halls, out the door, down the hill, and past the water tower.

Single file, folks moseyed through Room Five, picked up one item, and moved on. The Up Yonder kazoo band provided live entertainment. The PTA passed out free refreshments. And Mrs. McBloom got to personally shake hands with all her former students. (She bawled like a baby in wet britches.)

Heavens to belly buttons! The treasures pulled from the rubble were astounding! Long-lost works of art . . . important historical documents . . . and rare geological finds were rediscovered.

The Up Yonder parade of pickers went on plucking for hours. Among other things, they fished out four feathered quill pens, a potbellied stove, three buffalo nickels, a postcard signed by President Roosevelt, thirteen petrified cupcakes, a poodle shirt, a litter of kittens, a rotary-dial telephone, and a flag with forty-eight stars!

By sundown, Room Five was completely cleaned out. The apple tree was replanted next to the playground and dedicated to Mrs. McBloom.

Principal Pumpernickel awarded Georgia the prestigious Knickerbocker Whippersnapper Award for Excellence.

"Splendid use of your noggin, Miss Peachpit."

"Thank you, sir."

All in all, it was a mighty fine day for all the good folks of Up Yonder.

In the days that followed, the town held the granddaddy of all yard sales and sold all the knickknacks, critters, and whatnots that had been uncovered from Room Five. The money raised was used to send Mrs. McBloom on a fancy-schmancy cruise.

"Oh, higgly-piggly! Bless your hearts!"

"Bon voyage!"

As for sweet, young Miss Bumblesprout, she began her teaching career that fall in a gussied-up, spiffed-up, tidy Room Five.

"Good morning, class. Open your science books. Today we're going to plant pumpkin seeds!"

Why Possum's Tail Is Bare

by Gayle Ross

Long ago in the beginning days of the world, Possum didn't look the way he does now. Creator gave Possum a beautiful, bushy, furry tail, and Possum was vain about this tail. He bragged about it all the time and sang about it at every dance, until Rabbit (who didn't have much of a tail left since Bear had pulled his off) became jealous and decided to play a trick on Possum.

Rabbit went to the other animals and said, "Let's have an honor dance for Possum's tail." But all the other animals said, "We are tired of hearing Possum sing about his tail."

"If we have an honor dance for Possum," said Rabbit, "and we let him sing about his tail all night, perhaps he will not talk about it so much from now on." Well, the other animals said they had never thought about it quite like that, and maybe Rabbit was right. And so they agreed to have an honor dance for Possum's tail.

Rabbit traveled to Possum's house and gave him the news. "You mean I can sit where everyone can see me?" said Possum.

"Oh, yes." said Rabbit. "You will have a special seat of honor right next to the council fire."

"Do you mean I can sing and dance and talk about my tail all night?" asked Possum.

"Oh, yes." said Rabbit. "That's what the dance is for, to honor your beautiful tail!"

Well, of course this pleased Possum very much, and he said that he would come. Rabbit said, "I will send Cricket to you on the day of the dance to comb and brush the fur on your tail so it will look its best." Possum liked this idea as well.

So Rabbit went to Cricket, who is such an expert haircutter that the Cherokee word for him means "the barber." Rabbit told him exactly how to fix the hair on Possum's tail.

On the day of the dance, Cricket went to Possum's house. Possum stretched out and closed his eyes and Cricket began to comb and rush the fur on Possum's tail, until it was its silkiest and shiniest. "Possum," said Cricket, "I'm going to wind a red string around the fur of your tail, very very tight, all the way to the tip. It will keep the hair smooth until it is time for you to dance. Remember Possum, don't take the string off until just before you dance!"

That night, when the sun went down, the drums began to plan and the singers to call. Everyone gathered at the council house. Possum sat in a special seat of honor, right next to the council fire, where the light was brightest.

Soon, the other animals began to call, "Possum dance! Possum dance!" So Possum reached around behind him and pulled off the red string. With that, every hair on his tail fell off, but Possum didn't know it. He leaped into the circle of firelight and began to dance, singing, "See my beautiful bushy, furry tail!" The animals began to laugh. Possum sang, "See how it sweeps the ground!" And the animals laughed louder.

Possum decided maybe they hadn't heard him right, and so he sang louder, and the animals laughed harder.

Finally, Possum realized that something must be wrong. He looked around behind him, and instead of the beautiful bushy, furry tail that he had always known, there was a long, red, skinny, hairless tail. Possum was so surprised and humiliated, all he could do was fall to the ground and grin helplessly, which Possum still does whenever you take him by surprise. And Possum's grandchildren all have red, skinny, hairless tails to this very day.

The Great Divvy-Up

BY DON ABRAMSON

Well, you ask me what I think is a fair way to divide things up, to distribute them when you've got a lot of people laying claim. That's never been an easy question to answer. A lot of folks favor one method; a lot of folks favor another. My mother always used to avoid an argument between my brother and me over who got a bigger piece of cake. She'd have one of us cut the cake and the other one choose which piece to take.

But when you've got a whole lot more than one little cake? That puts me in mind of a story.

The village of Winsome Valley was small, but very pleasant, and the villagers all got along with each other fine. They were there to help each other if some cattle got loose and went astray, or if somebody's barn roof collapsed, or if somebody's son caught the flu. They'd share recipes, wrapping paper, and gossip. Just the kind of quiet little place you'd like to live in.

And they had no quarrels with each other—well, almost none. There was the time that Mrs. Prescott's cat walked across Mr. Arne's freshly painted back porch and then went to take a nap in Mrs. Stilton's laundry basket. But they settled that and ended up sharing a good laugh over it.

No, the time I'm talking about was much more serious than that, and it looked for a bit as if the good villagers of Winsome Valley were going to get all up-in-arms with each other. And it came about because of—a successful harvest. That was the year a lot of the families thought they'd get together and share their lands and share their crops.

In one section they planted potatoes, and either the land was right or the rain was right or the sun, but they found themselves with a bumper crop. So they shared the work of harvesting the potatoes, and after they put aside a number of potatoes for seed for next year, they looked at the huge pile of potatoes they had stacked upon the village green and smiled at each other with satisfaction.

Then somebody—I think it was Connie Chiming—somebody said, "Well, how do we divide them, now?"

The husbands and wives and children and grandparents all looked at each other and puzzled. How *should* they divide all those potatoes? See, it's one thing to divide up something loose, like grain. You just weigh it out, or measure it in cups. But the potatoes were—well, separate things.

"I think we need to know first," suggested Matt Meterson, "how many potatoes we're looking at, in all."

"Sounds reasonable," said Wanda Whist. "How do we find that out?"

"Let's count them," said Sam Stilton. And so they named three of their members to do the counting. That took quite a while, let me tell you. See, the three of them—George Gomer, Hanna Hadley, and Pete Prescott, decided they should each count the potatoes separately and then compare notes. It was a good thing they started out in the village green, because they really did need all that space. It went like this: George would take a potato out of the big community pile and put it in his own counting pile and say to himself, "one," and go back for another potato.

Then Hanna would take a potato out of George's pile and put it in her own counting pile and say to herself, "one," and go get another potato.

Except Hanna didn't trust herself not to lose track of the numbers, so she kept a tally on one of her son's yellow school tablets. Then it was Pete's turn to take a potato out of Hanna's pile and put it in his own counting pile and say to himself, "one," and go get another potato. Now, Pete didn't trust his own memory any more than Hanna did, so he kept a tally too. But Pete, he had his own methods, and for every potato he counted, he'd take a dried pea from a large sack of dried peas he had stored down cellar and put that pea in another sack, his counting sack.

These three official counters worked all day and well into the night, with neighbors helpfully holding flashlights for them to work by. Finally they finished counting. The huge pile of potatoes had been moved from the northeast corner of the village green to the northwest corner, to the southwest, to the southeast.

When all that was done, the villagers crowded around to find out how many potatoes they all shared. But George was too hoarse to talk (he'd been counting out loud, you see), and Pete realized he'd have to go home now and count his dried peas, which was going to keep him up *way* past his bedtime.

Then Hanna said, "Well, if we're going to have to wait until tomorrow to hear their counts, I guess mine can wait too." And so the villagers covered the potatoes with a great tarpaulin, and they all went home to bed.

The next morning they all gathered again, eager to learn their share of the potato crop.

Sam stood in front of them. "I counted 2,485 potatoes," he said hoarsely.

George shuffled up, yawning. "I counted 1,928 peas—er, potatoes," he said.

"You didn't lose some peas through a hole in your bag, did you?" quipped Arthur Arne. Some of the neighbors laughed.

"And I counted 2,631," stated Hanna, coming forward. "Well, what're we to do about this discrepancy?"

"We should have had Stu Stilton do the count," remarked Francine Fodor.

"He goes to college."

"Aw, Francine," answered Stu's father, Sam, "you know Stu's on a basketball scholarship. He's no better at math than I am."

Now Charles Chiming spoke up. "Anyway, I just tried dividing all three of those tallies, and they none of them come out even."

"Divided by what?" asked Mary Meterson.

"Why, eleven, of course," replied Charles. "There's eleven families here."

"That's true," put in Fred Fodor, thoughtfully, "but the families aren't equal. Look, Hiram and Hanna Hadley have got three sons and a daughter, that's six. But then there's Matt and Mary Meterson, they're only two, and Teresa Tesla lives alone."

"Well, then," asked Hiram Hadley, "How many *people* have we got?"

Two of the villagers did a quick head count, and miraculously, both of them arrived at the same figure: forty-six. But forty-six didn't go into the tally figures either.

"So what *are* we going to do?" asked Larry Lisle finally.

"We'll just have to count them all over again, I guess," sighed Polly Prescott.

"You know," began Teresa Tesla, "that does seem like a great deal of extra work, moving all those potatoes out of the pile they're in now to just another pile."

Now, the villagers respected Widow Tesla because she was the oldest person in the village, and the wisest. So they thought about what she'd said.

"But what should we do instead?" Asked William Whist. "We've got to divvy those potatoes somehow."

"Well, sure," Teresa answered. "But what if—what if, instead of counting all the potatoes and then dividing them, we just divided them?"

"What do you mean?" asked Sally Stilton.

Teresa continued, "One by one, the head of each family can come forward and take as many potatoes as there are family members. And then we'll repeat that and repeat that—through the whole pile."

Most of the villagers seemed to think that *was* a pretty good idea. Teresa *was* a wise old woman, after all, and they were just about to draw straws to see who would go first, when—

"Wait," said Lilith Lisle. "It's not fair. Look at those potatoes. They're all different sizes. Some are large, and some are small. Now, this one," she continued, pulling a potato from the pile, "could feed practically a whole family by itself."

"That's a good point," said Teresa. "Well, everybody, when you're making your choices, take the largest potatoes you can find. Then when we get down to the small ones, it'll still be fair."

So once again, the villagers prepared to draw straws, when—

"Wait," said Fred Fodor. "It's not fair. Think—Stu Stilton is in college, and he's away from home nine months of the year. He shouldn't count as a whole person here. Maybe only one-fourth."

Polly Prescott spoke up rather crossly, "Well, for that matter, Fred, your two little grandbabies can't possibly eat as much as a grown person. They shouldn't count as whole people either. Maybe a third each."

But Grace Gomer piped in angrily, "Now, that's just plain dumb! Here's my grandfather. His teeth are bad, and he doesn't eat much anyway. Do you want to count him as one-eighth of a person?"

And Grace's grandfather, whose teeth may have been bad but whose hearing wasn't, became enraged. "I won't stand for that, do you hear? It's not fair! I won't go for anything less than seven-eighths!" And he pounded the ground with his cane.

"Friends, neighbors—stop this!" Teresa cried. "Look at how silly we are all being. We should be here to celebrate our fine potato harvest, and here we are bickering over how much a person is worth. Now, admit it, the only fair way to do this is—one potato per person."

Well, I'm not sure how old Teresa Tesla managed to convince all of them, but as I said, she was the oldest and the wisest. Finally they agreed to do it her way, to choose one potato per person at a time until they'd gone through the whole pile.

And that worked fine, until—

"We're almost at the end," observed Mary Meterson.

"We *are* at the end," answered William Whist. "There aren't enough potatoes left for everyone to have another choice."

"But we've still got some potatoes left over," said Sally Stilton.

"Yes, there's still—twenty-seven potatoes left," Lilith Lisle said after a quick spud—count.

Connie Chiming wailed, "Now, how in the world can we divide *those*? With eleven families—"

"And forty-six people—" added her husband, Charles.

"No, now that's not hard at all," spoke up Teresa. "Look, give those twenty-seven potatoes to me—" Some grumblings were beginning to be heard among the villagers, but Teresa ignored them, and continued, smiling. "And tomorrow night, we'll have a village festival, a harvest celebration. And each family will bring a dish to share—like Wanda, you can bring your famous green-bean casserole. And I—I will bring a very large pot of mashed potatoes!"

Plant vs. Animal

BY DONNA O'MEARA

Look out for nectar thieves, leaf chompers, and seed eaters. Beware of grazers, root munchers, and sap suckers. Plants are under attack. Every animal around either eats plants or eats someone that does.

Almost every part of a plant, from its roots to its fruits to its leaves, is full of the nutrients living things need. The plant needs those nutrients, too. It has to protect itself against nibbling predators, but how? Plants can't run and hide. So they stay and fight—with thorns, disguises, poisons, and even secret messages. These defenses are impressive, but over time many animals have adapted with stunning counterattacks of their own.

Defense: Spikes, Thorns, Hairs

Walking through a garden, you bend over to smell a rose. Ahh! The perfume of a rose in bloom, the silky pink petals, the—Ouch! The thorns!

If you've ever been pricked by a rosebush, you have done battle with a basic form of plant defense. Lots of animals eat leaves, but leaves are vital to a plant's survival. Leaves capture sunlight and turn it into energy the plant needs to grow. Many plants protect their leaves with a sort of barbed-wire fence. A plant's pointy parts can be squat and thick, like rosebush thorns; long and narrow, like a cactus's spines; or filled with poison, like a nettle's hairs.

Tiny hairs deter insects that are small enough to eat their way around big thorns. Insects have a hard time landing on hairy leaves or climbing up a fuzzy stem—the hairs get in the way.

Counterattack

An acacia tree's branches are protected by two-inch thorns, but the long, long tongue of a giraffe can maneuver around the thorns to pick off tender leaves. And the inside of a giraffe's mouth is tough and leathery, so a stray thorn can't do much damage. Score one for the animals.

Defense: Armor

A suit of armor provides excellent protection. Just ask a knight. Or an oak. A tree's tough bark protects the soft wood underneath and seals in sap, which carries food and water. Even flowers have armor. The green leafy part at the base of the petals, called the calyx, protects a bud while it develops.

If you've ever tried to crack a walnut, you know that some seeds have the best armor of all. Seeds contain nutrients to feed the new plant. Hard shells protect the precious seeds inside from animals that want those nutrients for themselves. The seeds of the *Bertholletia* tree, also called Brazil nuts, are clustered inside the seed pod with a shell so strong, no animal can chew through it.

Counterattack

Well, no animal except the agouti. Brazil nuts are tough, but this rabbit-sized rodent is tougher.

It uses sharp teeth to chisel through the seed pod and break out the nuts inside. Then it eats some and buries the rest for later. Lucky for the tree, the agouti has a bad memory, and forgotten nuts grow into new trees. Score one for the plants.

Defense: Trapdoors and Disappearing Leaves

Plants are rooted to one spot, but that doesn't mean they can't move. *Mimosa pudica*, also called the sensitive plant, can quickly fold its leaves to hide them from predators. And snapdragon flowers have built-in trapdoors that snap shut to keep out unwanted insects. The snapdragon needs some insects to spread its pollen, and it attracts them with sweet nectar. But ants are so small and smooth they can steal nectar without being coated with pollen. To keep out such nectar thieves, a snapdragon's petals push tightly together, so a tiny ant can't get in.

Counterattack

The snapdragon's trapdoor doesn't keep out all nectar lovers. Fat, fuzzy bees are big enough to push their way between the flower's petals. As they sip nectar, they brush against pollen grains that they'll carry to the next snapdragon—which is what the flower wanted all along. Score one for the plants.

Defense: Poison

After hiking through the woods, you start to feel an itch on your ankle. You scratch and scratch, but the bumpy red rash just spreads. They don't call the plant that causes it poison ivy for nothing.

The oil that made you itch is so potent that leaves a hundred years old can still cause a rash.

Plants rely on an amazing arsenal of chemicals to defend themselves against predators. Some of these concoctions are among the deadliest poisons around. Eating just one seed from the castor bean plant could kill a small child. The poison in the milkweed plant can give a cow a heart attack.

The danger in making poisons strong enough to kill, however, is that your enemies will soon adapt. After all, the only animals left to reproduce will be the ones that can survive the poison, and they will pass on their immunity to their offspring. Also, plants need *some* animals and insects around to spread their seeds and pollen. So some smart plants make chemicals that don't kill predators but just turn the plant's leaves bitter and unappetizing—broccoli is one example.

Counterattack

Even a deadly poison doesn't keep away all insects. Monarch caterpillars are among the few creatures that can stomach the poison found in milkweed leaves. They actually store the poison in their bodies, as a toxic defense against their own predators. Score one for the animals.

Defense: Secret Messages

Some tricky plants fight back by attracting the enemies of insects that eat them. When a broccoli or Brussels sprout plant is invaded by sap-sucking aphids, it gives off a chemical that attracts tiny wasps. Each female wasp lays an egg inside an aphid. When the baby wasp hatches, it kills the aphid by eating it from the inside out.

How does the plant know it's being eaten by aphids? Scientists think that plants react to chemicals in the insects' spit.

When under attack from giraffes, acacia trees can't shout "Save yourselves!" But they can warn their neighbors with chemical signals carried on the wind. In response to the signal, acacias downwind from the tree that is being eaten pump their leaves full of bitter-tasting chemicals.

Counterattack

Smart giraffes don't bother with trees downwind. Instead they move upwind to find acacias that haven't been warned to make their leaves taste terrible. Score one for the animals.

Who Wins?

Plant defends itself against predator. Predator adapts to overcome the defense. So who wins? The war isn't over yet. The back-and-forth struggle between plants and the creatures that want to eat them has been going on for millions of years, and it'll keep evolving for millions more.

The Extreme Team

BY Pamela S. Turner

One survives in the blistering Australian desert. The other, deep in the frozen Arctic. They're part of the few. The proud. And the slimy.

It's summer in the Australian desert. The last puddles of rainwater are quickly disappearing under the burning sun. A tubby gray-green frog squats under the acacia bush, digging backwards. The heels of his back feet have special claws to help scrape away the dirt. After burying himself a foot underground, the Australian water-holding frog will use amazing tricks to survive for months—or years—until awakened by the next rains.

As heat rises in the southern hemisphere, cold grips the northern hemisphere. Eleven thousand kilometers away in Alaska, above the Arctic Circle, a wood frog burrows down into leaf litter. The mottled brown wood frog is the same size as the Australian water-holding frog (about 5 centimeters long). She'll use her own special tricks to survive winter as a frozen "frogsicle."

How long can a frog survive the extreme cold of the Arctic or the extreme heat of the desert? As strange as it may seem, both the North American wood frog and the Australian water-holding frog must solve the same problem. Both must find a way to resist *desiccation* (drying out). Regardless of whether it's evaporated in the dry desert heat or locked up in ice by the freezing cold, water lost can mean life lost for a moist frog.

"The Extreme Team" by Pamela S. Turner. From *Odyssey's* May 2002 issue: "Wanted Alive: Fragile Frogs," © 2002, Cobblestone Publishing, 30 Grove Street, Suite C, Peterborough, NH 03458. All rights reserved. Used by permission of Carus Publishing Company.

A Tomb and a Cocoon

The water-holding frog uses the desert earth as his first line of defense. Yet even his insulating burrow is not enough protection from the desert sun. The water-holding frog also begins shedding several layers of skin. The skin gradually hardens, becoming a waterproof cocoon that keeps moisture inside. The cocoon covers the entire frog, except for two small breathing holes. The water-holding frog becomes dormant. He hardly breathes and his heart barely beats, but he is still alive in his desert tomb.

Even with a tomb and a cocoon, a desert frog needs as much water as possible to survive. The water-holding frog stores large quantities of water—more than his own weight—in his bladder and in pockets under his skin. Asleep in his cocoon, he can stay moist for a long time. In some parts of the Australian desert, it may not rain for several years.

Eventually, rain comes again. The water soaks down through the hard-baked earth, awakening the water-holding frog. He eats his way out of his cocoon and digs up to the surface. Other frogs emerge, and quickly begin breeding in the wet "frog heaven" created by spring and summer rainstorms.

A Living Ice Cube

The North American wood frog lives farther north than any other reptile or amphibian. The wood frog's neighbors—arctic hares, caribou, and wolves—use fur coats as protection from freezing, but not the moist little frog. The wood frog's motto seems to be, "If you can't beat 'em, join 'em." Rather than fighting the deep freeze, the wood frog becomes an ice cube.

The cells and body cavities of living creatures contain a lot of fluid. During freezing, ice forms both inside an animal's cells and in the spaces outside cells but inside the body (like the stomach cavity). Ice inside a living cell can slice, tear, or burst the cell apart. (Ouch!) Ice forming inside body cavities pulls water from surrounding cells. As those cells lose their water, they dry out (desiccate) and collapse.

Most animals die quickly under these circumstances—but not the wood frog. When she feels the first chill of winter, the wood frog burrows under the leaf litter on the forest floor. Her liver begins to work overtime, making huge amounts of a sugary chemical called *glucose*. Her heart pumps faster, spreading the glucose quickly through her small body.

As the temperature drops, the wood frog's body fluids begin to freeze. Ice forms first inside the large spaces in her body. The water in these spaces has impurities—tiny pieces of dust or bacteria—that "jump-start" ice crystal growth. As ice forms inside the wood frog's body cavities, it pulls water from surrounding cells. Because the sugary glucose can't pass as easily across the cell wall, it keeps the wood frog's cells from drying out and collapsing. She may have a belly full of ice, but her heart, brain, and other organs are full of slushy glucose. The wood frog can survive even when 65 percent of her body fluids are frozen solid.

The wood frog's body shuts down completely. While frozen, she has no heartbeat, no breathing, and no measurable brain activity. Yet, when spring arrives, the frogsicle bounces back to life, and out into another wet "frog heaven" created by all that melted snow and ice!

Treasures of the Sierra

BY AARON DERR

The Scouts of Troop 14, San Francisco, California, have some time to kill.

They drove 100 miles this July morning, and they're ready to begin their four-day backpacking trek across northern California's High Sierra.

But a truck carrying food and supplies has broken down somewhere along the way. So now the guys must stand around the parking lot and wait . . . and wait. Then assistant Scoutmaster John Muir Laws, a wildlife biologist and illustrator, has an idea.

In addition to backpacking, the guys are here to help Laws edit his series of guidebooks covering Sierra plants and wildlife.

So why not start now?

Minutes later, they're only a few yards from the parking lot, but they might as well be in another world.

A handful of aquatic garter snakes dart across the surface of a pond.

There's a mountain chickadee sending out its unique call that sounds an awful lot like "cheeeeeseburger."

They come across a western juniper, with its furry, peeling bark.

"Treasures of the Sierra" by Aaron Derr, *Boys' Life*, July 2006. Reprinted by permission of Aaron Derr and *Boys' Life*, July 2006, published by the Boy Scouts of America.

The Scouts note that a rough copy of Laws's guidebook doesn't mention the unique bark, but it does mention the presence of berries. Not so fast, the Scouts say. There are no berries on this tree.

Laws nods and jots down some notes.

Minutes later, the group stumbles across a patch of wandering daisies.

The Scouts note that they look different from the illustration in the book.

So Laws sits and draws them over again.

The editing process has begun.

"That one truck coming in two-and-a-half hours late got everybody bored," says 14-year-old Brady Borcherding, a Star Scout. "But once we started going, everybody realized how great this was going to be."

Bring Only What You Need

What the Scouts realized on the edge of the parking lot is the same lesson they learned throughout their 30-mile hike: There's some amazing stuff going on in the trees, on the ground, and in the air. You just have to know where to look.

But that doesn't mean this is just one big easy-going nature hike. The trail will take them up to 8,500 feet, where there is still some snow on the ground in July despite daytime temperatures in the 70s.

You can tell the experienced backpackers from the inexperienced ones by the weight of their backpacks.

"You have to learn how to limit what you bring," say 15-year-old Life Scout Peter Nedeau.

"There are things that you see at home that you might think you need, but you really don't need them. That's the key."

"People are wondering why my backpack is so much lighter than theirs."

Because of the late start, the group has to make up some time in the next few days. They backpack a full eight hours sometimes, and the first couple of days are mostly uphill as the air gets thinner and thinner.

One particular stretch sees the boys head up an incline that seems to go on forever. They play it safe and zigzag back and forth instead of trying to go straight up.

It would be a challenge even without packs.

"My favorite part was when we got to the top and we could just see everything," Peter says.

This trail takes the group through the Eldorado National Forest, the Stanislaus National Forest, and the Mokelumme Wilderness, and it seems you can see all three from the top. But after a short break, the guys have their packs back on and are headed down the other side.

Star Scout Eric Gordon, 14, is hiking near the back of the group, where they're having more nature discussions than up front. Now, he's come across a bit of a mystery. He and some fellow Scouts are examining very long, winding "tubes" of dirt that appear to have been placed perfectly intact on top of the ground.

How did such perfect tubes form?

Laws knows, but he isn't telling . . . for now.

A Rare Find

One morning, some of the Scouts are awakened at sunrise by the sound of a woodpecker. They pop out of their tents and head over to investigate.

Turns out it's a black-backed woodpecker. Laws is elated because these birds normally live only in areas affected by forest fires. This one has a nest full of babies.

"Waking up and seeing a woodpecker that Jack had seen only once before was pretty cool," Brady says, calling Laws by his nickname. "Its species is on the decline, and for this area, it was pretty rare because this isn't a fire-scorched forest."

In one open field, the group crowds around some wildflowers and helps Laws identify them from the field guide.

The flowers are yellow, so they turn to the yellow section of the books.

There are four petals per flower, so they turn to the section that features four-petaled flowers.

First guess: A California broom.

Not quite.

Next guess: A Western Wallflower.

Bingo.

A Scout notes that the books says these flowers look different depending on the elevation in which they're growing, but it doesn't fully explain the difference.

Laws nods and jots down more notes.

Before the day is done, Eric is demanding an answer to the mystery of the tubes of dirt.

The answer: gophers.

During the summer, they dig through the ground and kick up dirt everywhere.

But during the winter, they dig tunnels through the snow and into the ground, and the dirt that they excavate from the ground gets pushed back through the snow tunnels.

When the snow melts, the dirt sinks down onto the ground, never losing its perfect tube shape.

Eric seems satisfied and vows to stick to the back of the group with hopes of finding more answers.

"It's going great in the back," he says. "We're doing more nature stuff, which is nice."

My Baja Adventure

BY TATI, AS TOLD TO ELIZABETH SCHLEICHERT

I just went with my family on the most *amazing* trip ever! Where to? Baja (BAH-hah) California. As I found out, *baja* is Spanish for *lower*. But Lower California is actually in Mexico.

Baja is unlike any other place I've seen. It's nearly surrounded by water. Along the coast I saw piles of dark, jumbled-up rocks. Those rocks made me feel as if I'd landed on the moon! Even spookier, I heard pirates once roamed the area. Maybe there's some buried treassure there! But I wanted to discover another Baja treasure: its wildlife.

My mom and I had heard that Baja's surrounding seas were teaming with wildlife. So off we set in a kayak to try and find some.

Gliding along quietly, we soon came upon a few brown pelicans. Later, it was cool to see one flying overhead. But it didn't stay in the air very long. All of a sudden it plunged bill-first into the water to scoop up some fish.

We also spied a handsome sea lion resting on the rocks. It seemed almost tame, turning to look at us if posing.

Next, we went ashore to explore Baja's white, sandy beaches. And that's where my new friend, Thomas, and I stumbled across a sea star. A mighty wave must have tossed it high up on land.

"My Baja Adventure" by Tati, as told to Elizabeth Schleichert. Reprinted from the April 2007 issue of *Ranger Rick*® magazine, with the permission of the publisher, the National Wildlife Federation®.

We felt how soft and bumpy it was. Then we turned it over and admired the tiny tube feet on the undersides of its arms. These help the sea star walk along the rocky ocean floor. After a while, Thomas and I put the sea star back in the water. We didn't want it to die in the hot sun.

As we continued down the beach, we saw colorful shells and bits of coral as well as the dried-white bones of dead fish scattered everywhere. There were a lot of sea urchin skeletons, too. Most of them were broken, but then we found a perfect one. It was a beauty! When it was alive, stubby spines stuck out everywhere. Now we saw bumps instead.

Of all my Baja adventures, nothing could top what happened one special day—the day we went out whale-watching. Gray whales spend the winter in Baja's shallow waters. There they mate, and many of the females give birth to calves. I just hoped I'd see some!

Turns out, I didn't have long to wait. A gray whale twice as long as our boat surfaced right next to us. And guess what—it stuck around long enough for me to lean over and touch it!

As the whale started to sink beneath the surface, it rolled over on its back. I could see its two long *throat pleats*. (These, I was told, let the throat expand while the whale is feeding.)

Wow! How could anything top that day?

I was sad when it was time to head home. But I hoped to go back before long to discover even more Baja treasures.

Read Aloud Anthology

Why the Sun Comes Up When Rooster Crows

BY MARTHA HAMILTON AND MITCH WEISS

Long ago, when the world was young, there wasn't just one sun in the sky. There were nine. Their blazing heat scorched the land. The earth grew hotter and hotter. The crops shriveled. People began to die.

The people tried to think of ways to block the heat of the nine suns. Finally, they decided to ask their best archer to shoot the suns out of the sky. He listened to their plan and agreed to help.

The next morning before sunrise, the archer climbed to the top of the highest mountain. As each sun appeared, he strung an arrow and, one by one, shot the suns. He did this eight times until there was only one sun left. As the last sun watched what happened to her sisters, she grew more and more terrified. She hid behind a mountain so that she would not be pierced by an arrow.

At first the people celebrated their victory. They praised the archer for his great skill. But they soon realized that they couldn't live without the sun. The world was now freezing cold. Nothing would grow. They called out to the hidden sun, but no matter what they said, she wouldn't come out.

A great meeting was called to decide what to do. "We just find someone who can convince the sun that we mean no harm."

A few people suggested Tiger. They said, "Tiger is a powerful animal. His words will be believed by the sun."

But Tiger's voice was so loud and sounded so much like a growl that the sun grew even more frightened.

One of the village elders spoke up. "Perhaps we need an animal that has a soothing voice. Why not ask Oriole? No one sings better than Oriole."

Oriole sang her sweetest song. Although the sun liked Oriole's singing, she still wouldn't come out. Many other birds tried, but none of them succeeded.

At last, another of the elders suggested Rooster. He argued, "It's true that Rooster doesn't sing as beautifully as Oriole, but he's fearless and won't give up." When the people asked Rooster, he didn't hesitate. He strutted to the top of the mountain and called out, "Cock-a-doodle-doo!"

The sun was too scared to come out. Rooster crowed a second time, "Cock-a-doodle-doo!" A tiny bit of sun peeked out from behind the mountain. She was still afraid that she would be shot with an arrow. When the Rooster crowed a third time, the sun was convinced that it was safe. Her fear vanished, and she came out from behind the mountain in her full glory.

The crowd cheered. The sun was very pleased with their reaction. She was grateful to Rooster for finally convincing her to come out. To reward him she took a bit of red out of the morning sky, made it into the shape of a comb, and placed it on top of Rooster's head.

To this day, Rooster is very proud that he saved the world. If you watch him in the barnyard, you will see that he struts about with his chest puffed out and the bright red comb on his head. And every morning when Rooster crows, the sun soon appears.

The Quarrel Between Earth and Sky

EDITED BY SUSAN CANTOR

There are many stories to explain how the earth became separated from the sky. In this Yoruba story from western Nigeria, the consequences of the sky withdrawing explain there are periods of drought and famine.

Long ago, Earth and Sky were best of friends. They considered themselves equals in everything, and never quarreled. They often spent all day together, which they greatly enjoyed, especially when hunting.

One day they went into the bush to hunt. They followed the trails of antelope and deer, they tracked wild pigs, and they looked for birds, but their hunt was not successful. As the day wore on, they got more and more hungry, and they became rather irritable. Finally, at sunset, they caught a little bush rat. It wasn't really enough to feed two hungry hunters, but it was all they had. They made a fire and roasted the bush rat, but when it was ready to eat, an argument broke out.

Earth said, "I will eat the first portion because I am senior to you. In the beginning, Earth was there before the Sky came into existence."

"That's not true!" Sky retorted. "Sky was here long before Earth was formed so I should be given the first portion."

They continued to argue about who should be given the first portion, neither giving in to the other, and the more they argued, the more bitter their feelings became. At last Sky said, "This is no way to treat me. You aren't my friend anymore, so why should I be yours? I don't want your company any longer. Keep your bush rat—I hope you enjoy it!" And Sky stormed off. He went high up, far above the Earth and stayed there. Earth was angry, too, and left the place, leaving the bush rat lying there uneaten.

Before this quarrel, when Earth and Sky were close friends, rains were plentiful, rivers were always full, and the earth was always fertile. Vegetables and green things grew, the bush was abundant with game, crops flourished, and harvests were good. All creatures lived an easy life.

But once Sky moved far away, rains became scarce, the rivers dried up, the earth turned dry, and deserts spread across the land. Wells dried up, crops failed, the animals of the bush began to die out, and people began to starve.

A meeting was called of all he creatures of the bush to see what could be done. The dead bush rat, the cause of all the trouble, was brought before them. They decided to appease Sky. A messenger would be chosen to carry the bush rat to Sky as a present, and beg Sky to come back down near Earth.

The birds were asked to select one of their own to carry the gift. One of them was chosen, but he was unable to carry the bush rat high enough to reach Sky. Another one tried and also failed. One after the other, all the strongest fliers among the birds were sent, but none of them were strong enough to carry the bush rat to Sky. At last Vulture spoke.

"I can fly higher than any of you. Let me carry the bush rat to Sky."

The other creatures laughed, for Vulture was rather clumsy.

"If our best fliers can't do it, how do you suppose you can?" they demanded.

But Vulture insisted, and since everyone else had tried, they gave him the bush rat to carry. As he flew up toward the sky, Vulture sang:

> *Earth and Sky went hunting,*
> *Killed a bush rat for their meal.*
> *Earth claimed he was senior*
> *But Sky did not agree.*
> *Sky went far up high above*
> *Then Earth became quite dry.*
> *Yams stopped growing in the fields*
> *And maize lost all its grains.*
> *Mothers searched for water*
> *While their babies cried with thirst.*

As Vulture sang this song, flying higher and higher, Sky heard him. Sky was sorry at what was happening and decided to forget his anger. He accepted the gift of the bush rat from Vulture and in return gave Vulture a bag of magic red powder. Sky explained to Vulture that whenever rain was needed, he had only to scatter a tiny amount of this magic powder in the air, and rain would fall in abundance.

Vulture gladly took the bag of magic powder and began his long descent back down to Earth. On the way, however, he became more and more curious to see the powder, and couldn't stop himself from opening the bag to have a look.

Suddenly, a gust of wind blew the powder everywhere, scattering all of it into the air at once. Instantly the light faded, big black clouds covered the sun, and strong winds whipped through the air. The powerful winds broke the trees and blew down the houses. The torrents of rain came crashing down and great floods surged across the land, washing away crops and villages and leaving behind ruins.

When the storm was finally over, the creatures of the Earth looked for Vulture everywhere to ask him what had happened. At last they found him. He told them about his meeting with Sky, and the magic red powder he had been given. Then he explained his unfortunate accident. Everyone was furious. They attacked Vulture and beat him severely around the head.

As a result, Vulture, who used to have a beautiful set of head feathers, wound up with a bald head, which he has had ever since. The others, however, never got over their anger, and Vulture has never again been welcome among other animals. He has had to live apart from them, and is not allowed to share their food, but must wait until they are finished before eating their leftovers.

Wildlife Watching

BY JIM ARNOSKY

The woods were rain-soaked. Soil gurgled under the press of my footsteps. I walked a familiar trail, wide-eyed for a glimpse of wildlife. Ahead, something moved on the soggy leaves. It was a little snake! I tried to get a closer look, but it scooted behind a fallen tree branch. I approached again, very slowly, and knelt a few feet from the broken branch. The snake didn't move. It was an olive-colored garter snake with bright yellow stripes down its back. Each of its scales was "keeled" in the center by a raised line. The snake's eyes looked like polished stones. They made me wonder what they were seeing. Its delicate head was jade green and its mouth was white. A tiny forked tongue flicked out. It was dark red.

The little snake had sensed my approach and was seeking cover when I spotted it. Once behind the branch, it felt hidden, so it stayed, even when I came near. One secret to getting close to small, shy animals is to let them find cover before trying to approach them.

Wild animals are sensitive to everything around them. Stalking them takes practice and patience. In reptiles, fish, and mammals, the sense of smell is acute. A snake depends on its sense of smell to locate food and detect danger. A salmon can smell a bear in the water a mile upstream. A fox can sniff a rabbit's scent in tracks that are days old.

From *Secrets of a Wildlife Watcher* by Jim Arnosky. Copyright © 1983 Jim Arnosky. Reprinted by arrangement with Jim Arnosky and Susan Schulman, A Literary Agency, New York.

Wherever you go you leave some of your scent in microscopic molecules that are released from your body and clothing. These molecules fall to the ground as you move. They cling to vegetation. They float in the air and drift to surrounding areas. Often your scent reaches an animal long before you do, which scares it away. When you see a wild animal, stay downwind. This will keep your scent in back of you and away from the animal you are watching.

Most animals can hear as well as they can smell. Even snakes, fish, and others deaf to airborne sounds can feel noises vibrating through the ground. When stalking wildlife, be as quiet as possible Step softly. Try not to scrape against trees or brush. If you must make a sound, do so when the animal you are watching is busy chewing food, shifting position, or moving to a new spot. It will be making noises of its own and may not notice yours. If you are heard and the animal becomes alert—freeze in your tracks!

Keep still and most animals will not see you, even if you are out in the open. In general, animals look out for movements. Many animals, including most mammals, see only in shades of gray. A motionless figure is difficult for them to single out of a scene. Sometimes the shape of a standing human, still or moving, will frighten them. You can disguise your human shape simply by crouching down.

I was once crouched downwind from a beaver who was working away on its dam. At times the busy engineer was less than ten feet from me.

It rolled some heavy stones to the dam site and shoved them into place with the side of its strong body. I could hear the stones squish into the mud on the dam. In my motionless crouch, I was invisible. After a while, though, my legs became stiff and I had to stand and stretch them. Instantly, the beaver saw me and disappeared under water with a loud splash of its flat tail.

When you witness an intimate tidbit of a wild animal's private life, glean all you can from the experience. Pay attention to the details, and wonder about what you see. Exercise your eyesight. Don't just look. Observe.

Sensing the Night

BY DIANA KAPPEL-SMITH

It was a spring evening in New Jersey, and Juana didn't want to go in for dinner. Last night she'd seen a raccoon in the yard, and she wanted to see if it would come back. Her older brother, Romero, had already called her twice.

"Juana, now!" he called with finality.

With a sign, Juana went indoors.

"What did you call that raccoon again?" Romero asked her as she sat down. "'Creepy-peculiar'?"

"The word is 'crepuscular,' Romero. Crepuscular means active-at-dawn-and-dusk. Don't act so dumb!"

"What does 'nocturnal' mean then, smarty-pants?" Romero asked.

"It means active at night, in the real dark. Like toads are, or opossums, or cockroaches. You're the one who told me that!"

"What do you say we go down to the pond after dinner, when it gets dark, and see if any toads are singing," Romero said. Actually, he knew a lot more about wildlife than his 10-year-old sister do. He was a biology student in college.

"In the dark?" Juana asked eagerly. "Sure. Fine. Let's go," she said. "But don't tease me anymore."

The pond to which they often went was in the woods. Juana had never been there in the dark. It held water only in the spring. Because of that, no fish lived there.

Romero said it was called a *vernal* pool. Many *amphibians* lay their eggs in vernal pools, because no fish are there to eat them.

Romero and Juana knew the pond well and didn't take a flashlight because Romero said that peoples' eyes only adapt to the dark if they don't use a light. At first Juana was nervous as she stumbled along in the dark, but soon she could see the path, the trees, even ripples in the water.

"You're right! I can see really well!" she whispered to her older brother. "Only no colors. Just black and white."

"What . . . You didn't believe me?" Romero whispered back.

They saw three bats hunting over the pond, flittering shapes dark against the sky. These were probably big brown bat, the first to return north in the spring. Once in a while, a bat would zigzag as it caught an insect.

Nocturnal bats "see" in the dark by using *echolocation*. They make loud, high-pitched squeaks in the frequency range known as ultrasound that people can't hear. The sound bounces back from trees, rocks, and insects. With their large ears, and in some species their leaf-shaped nostrils, bats sense the shapes of things from their echoes.

Juana's mother had told her that bats were not the only creatures that use echolocation. Dolphins, seals, and porpoises use it to find prey in the deep sea. Some birds that live in caves also echolocate. These include the South American oilbird, whose "clicks" can be heard even by the human ear.

Juana and Romero sat quietly by the pool. They saw ripples, and then they heard loud burping sounds.

Juana tried not to giggle. Toads sounded so weird! Then they heard a different call, a high wheep-wheep, like a tiny bell. Peepers!

Peeper frogs are less than a couple of inches long, but their calls are very loud. Male toads and frogs were singing to call females to come to mate with them.

While the siblings sat there, they heard a gargly whistle from overhead.

"Screech owl!" Romero whispered. "That's really cool!"

Juana realized that the male owl was calling to tell other male screechies to stay away. This was his territory.

She also knew that some owls have eyes so large that there is no room in their skull for eye muscles, so they turn their whole heads to see around them. Other owls can hunt by hearing alone. With their sensitive ears, they can hear the movement of a mouse in the grass.

Suddenly, Juana heard a crashing in the leaves. She jumped.

"What's that?" she whispered, grabbing her Romero's jacket.

"Deer!" her brother said, but he had grabbed her jacket, too.

In the suburbs, deer have learned to be crepuscular. After people have gone indoors, deer come close to houses to eat people's plants.

And Romero decided that maybe it was time for them to call it a night too, since they both had school in the morning. On the way home, Romero told Juana that right now the sky was full of migrating birds, flying across the whole continent from South America, Mexico, even Antarctica. They were going as far as Greenland and northern Canada.

Most of the mammals that Juan and Romero saw in their neighborhood were crepuscular: cottontail rabbits, raccoons, skunks, foxes, rats, *feral* (wild) cats, and deer. These animals use smell as a language. They also have night-adapted eyes. One night, Juana saw the red shine of a coyote's eyes as it trotted along the hedge. Crepuscular mammals and some reptiles, such as alligators, have a mirror like layer called a *tapetum* behind their eyes. This reflects light back through the retina, doubling the light that can be sensed. When a light catches an animal at night, you sometimes see its bright "eyeshine." What looks like black dark to us looks like twilight to them, Juana thought.

But the most exciting thing she had learned tonight was that she could see pretty well in the dark herself.

"Maybe I'm crepuscular, too," she thought. "Hey, that's a good excuse not to come in for dinner!"

Fiddler Crabs to Rhinos

by George W. Frame

"Ouch!" I jerked my finger out of the fiddler crab's burrow in the black mud. Hanging on was a little fiddler, with its outsized pincers biting into my finger.

At the time, I was four years old, exploring with my grandfather. I held up my finger for him to see. "I guess this one didn't know me, Grandpop." I said.

My grandfather carefully pried open the big yellow pincers, relieving my pain. The fiddler scurried back to its burrow.

I was lucky. My family had a cottage that stood on pilings in the New Jersey salt marsh, within sight of the ocean. We went there to escape the stifling summer heat of the Philadelphia area.

My parents sat on the porch enjoying the sea air. I lay for hours on a rickety boardwalk, peering through the spaces between the boards and studying the water below. There I saw a world that my parents never noticed.

Everywhere I saw life and action. I could hardly bear to leave this world in the marsh when my mother called me to supper.

Back in the city, I liked school, especially science class. I rode my bicycle long distances to collect and identify tree leaves for a science project.

I sifted the soil behind my garage because my teacher said I would find at least ten different kinds of animals there. The creatures were all very tiny, of course, but I was amazed at how much life there was right in my backyard.

For the first two years of college I took lots of chemistry and physics classes. They were interesting, but I couldn't stay excited about laboratories and test tubes. I wanted to work out-of-doors.

Off to Africa

I couldn't wait any longer to see Africa and its wildlife, so I joined the Peace Corps and went to East Africa. There I worked in the wilderness, where I helped to plan pipelines to bring clean drinking water to villages.

I loved Africa, but I seemed to be getting no closer to realizing my dream of becoming a field biologist. Then something happened that changed my life.

Nearby, a biologist was studying the ecology of the black rhinoceros. He needed assistants to find and watch the huge beasts and to tranquilize them so that tags could be put on their ears.

He asked the Peace Corps for helpers. A few days later, the boy who had met a determined little fiddler crab so many years ago was now a young man, helping to hold a groggy one-ton rhino while the scientist clipped a bright tag to its ear. It was the turning point in my career. Suddenly I found what I had been looking for.

I returned to college and studied until I received a doctoral degree in wildlife ecology.

During those years I worked in the field, studying rhinos, cheetahs, African wild dogs, and Alaskan bears. I studied other things, too, from worms to forests.

Catastrophe

In 1972, I went back to Africa as a scientist ready to begin field research.

Poachers were killing more and more rhinos. By 1978, my wife and I were astounded to see dozens of dead rhinos, which had been killed illegally for their valuable horns. Almost all of the rhinos that had lived in this place were now gone.

I realized then that learning about an animal is not enough to save it. I decided to work to show others why wildlife is worth caring about and to help them understand the need for conservation.

I also set out to help find ways for villagers living near protected areas to earn money and benefit in other ways from wildlife conservation. I hoped to help change these people's thinking and their situations so that rhinos—and wild dogs and many other endangered animals would be more valuable to them alive than dead. In several cases, we have succeeded.

As a result, my work includes much more than field research. I also do a great deal of writing, speaking, and problem solving with communities.

No matter where I go, my heart always brings me back to the salt marsh. That's where I am now, on the boardwalk, in the same place where I spent so many hours as a child. I am happy to say that the natural world still survives here.

Flying Moose

BY JEFF IVES

Rocky Mountain moose are on the move—and they're flying first-class. Wildlife workers are using helicopters to send Utah's moose to Colorado. In exchange, wildlife officials in Colorado are capturing bighorn sheep to send to Utah. The animal swap is part of a plan to keep the moose and sheep populations in both states healthy.

One of the largest moose hauls took place in January 2007, when a single helicopter team captured 24 of the animals in a day. The moose are now roaming free in the Grand Mesa National Forest in Colorado, where the appearance of calves indicates that the moose population is growing. Colorado workers planned to hold up their end of the bargain by capturing 20 bighorn sheep to send to Utah in February 2007.

"This year was a major group move," [said] Stephanie Duckett, a biologist with the Colorado Division of Wildlife. Biologists are scientists who study living things. Duckett works at Grand Mesa, which didn't have any moose two years ago. "So far we have moved 90 moose to the mesa," she said. Most of those animals came from Weber County, Utah, where the moose population is in trouble.

The moose in northern Utah are threatened by overpopulation. That means there are too many animals for the environment to feed and support. Overpopulation can lead to animal starvation and disease. "It's bad for the population and bad for the environment," says Duckett.

Wildlife officials often try to prevent overpopulation by issuing permits that allow hunters to kill more animals during hunting season. That wasn't an option with Utah's moose; many of them live on private land where hunting is prohibited, or not allowed. Instead, wildlife officials decided to make a trade.

"Here in northern Utah, we have too many moose, and we've lost a lot of our bighorn sheep population," Utah wildlife manager Justin Dolling [said]. Colorado had a healthy supply of bighorn sheep to send to Utah and Colorado had plenty of room for Utah's extra moose.

Once they had a plan, wildlife officials had to find a way to safely catch the wild moose—one of the largest animal species in North America. They turned to animal-capture expert James Innes and his experienced team of helicopter "moose muggers." A moose mugger is an animal worker trained to capture a moose without harming it. "We have zero tolerance for inhumane (cruel) treatment of animals," Innes [said].

Innes's helicopter chases a moose into a clearing by flying over the forest before dropping a net to catch the animal. Once the moose is down, a moose mugger jumps out of the hovering helicopter and secures the animal's legs. "You have to use every trick in the book to tie them up," says Innes.

Once the moose is secured, it is placed in a canvas bag that hangs from the helicopter and then flown to base camp. There, a veterinarian, or animal doctor, gives the moose a checkup before it is placed on a truck and taken to its final destination—Grand Mesa.

The Resilient River

BY EMILY ZINK KIRCHNER

Miguel paddled faster to keep up with his mom. "I like canoeing, Mom. But this is hard work."

"It's a fun way to see the city, isn't it?" his mom answered.

"I like going under the bridges best," Miguel said.

Miguel and his mom are canoeing on the Chicago River. Their guide is leading a group of canoes on a tour with Friends of the Chicago River. Suddenly the guide motioned for them to stop.

"Look! There's a beaver! You don't normally see them in the daylight," said the guide. "Beavers are just returning to the area. They haven't lived here in about 150 years!"

"Where did they go?" asked Miguel.

"Pollution and people reduced their numbers and drove them out," explained the guide. "A long time ago, the Chicago area had swamplands and marshes. Beavers, foxes, minks, even bears, lived here. But when people decided to settle in the area, most of the wetlands were drained, and water pollution became a big problem."

"Was it really that bad?" asked Miguel.

"One section of the river on the South side is known as 'bubbly creek.' Do you know how it got the name 'bubbly creek'?"

"No," replied Miguel. "How?"

"In the early 1900s, there weren't many regulations for industry, so businesses in the area just dumped their waste into the river."

"Ewwwww!" said Miguel, squinching up his nose.

"What a mess!" exclaimed Miguel's mom.

"It was pretty gross. The river was only about a mile long and not very wide at that part, so the water and the waste was stagnant, or not moving. The waste in the river would decompose, or rot, and that caused the water to bubble up at the surface," the guide continued. "There's even a photo of a chicken standing on the water because the pollution was so thick. One writer said the water looked like lava!"

"I would NOT want to canoe through that," Miguel stated. He looked down at the water and frowned.

"I don't think it would be safe to canoe through that!" The guide went on. "While that section of the river is still called 'bubbly creek,' it's much healthier today. Fish and other animals are back, but in dry weather, the creek stops flowing. Then the fish have a hard time breathing. People are still working to improve that area."

The guide stopped for a moment. The group watched the beaver climb onto shore and disappear into the brush.

"The main part of the river downtown was also badly polluted at that time," the guide said. "The sludge was so thick at the surface that it caught fire during the Great Chicago Fire in 1871. Imagine seeing flames coming out of the water!"

"I bet people hoped all the pollution would burn away!" Miguel said. "So, is *this* water safe to canoe in?" he asked, looking at the water suspiciously.

"Yes, this water is safe to canoe in," the guide said firmly. "The river is no longer polluted like that."

"How did they get rid of all the pollution?" asked Miguel's mother.

"Well, it was a lot of work! Part of the problem was that the river was a slow and shallow prairie stream. When the city grew, the river was used for more and more things: commerce, transportation, drainage of swamplands, and even waste removal. The water became polluted, and the sluggish river wasn't powerful enough to take the pollution anywhere. Most of it moved slowly into Lake Michigan."

"So the whole river was smelly and gross?" Miguel asked.

"It was known at that time as 'the stinking river.' What does that tell you?" asked the guide. "What was worse," he continued, "was that people in Chicago got their drinking water from the lake. So the river would bring pollution to the lake, and the drinking water became tainted from the pollution. Many people got sick, and some died."

"Uggg! I'm never drinking water again!" Miguel said, and he leaned over the side of the canoe. "Bleck!"

"That was many years ago, Miguel," said his mom. "Water from the tap is very safe to drink now. Don't be dramatic!" She turned to the guide. "So what did the city do?" she asked.

"The city tried many solutions to the problem," explained the guide. "They tried to collect drinking water from farther out in Lake Michigan, away from the slow-moving Chicago River. But the population grew and so did the amount of pollution. The drinking water was tainted again," the guide said.

"Bleck!" Miguel gagged again. The guide ignored him and continued. "The city decided to do something drastic. Around 1900, engineers planned out how to change the flow of the river. After several attempts, they actually made the Chicago River flow backwards!"

"You can do that?" asked Miguel, straightening back up.

"They did," said the guide.

"How do you make a river flow backwards?" asked Miguel's mom.

"It's very complicated!" said the guide. "Let's see if I can explain it."

"The South Branch of the Chicago River used to start in a marsh called Mud Lake, south of Chicago, and flow toward the city and out into Lake Michigan. So the starting point, or source, of the South Branch was Mud Lake. Are you with me so far?" the guide asked Miguel.

"Yes, the starting point of the South Branch was Mud Lake." Miguel said.

"Good," said the guide. "So the engineers wanted to make Lake Michigan the source of the river. They wanted it to flow away from the city through Mud Lake to the Mississippi River, taking the pollution with it. Understand?"

"Yep," Miguel nodded.

"To do this, engineers made a new section of the river called a canal. They dug the canal through Mud Lake to drain all the water. They extended the canal to the rivers that flow into the Mississippi River.

Since water flows downhill, they dug the canal very deep, lower than the level of Lake Michigan. So now gravity pulls water from Lake Michigan into the South Branch, where it flows in the canal through what used to be Mud Lake, and then out to the rivers, finally ending up in the Mississippi."

"This is very complicated!" Miguel's mom said.

"But that way, the pollution stopped flowing into Lake Michigan. The waste was taken away from where Chicago gets drinking water."

Miguel was confused. "But didn't that just send the pollution somewhere else?" he asked.

"You're right. And people downstream were not happy about the project, but they couldn't stop it," the guide said. "Fortunately, in the 1930s, we learned how to treat wastewater to make the water safe again, so that cut down on the amount of pollution sent downstream to the Mississippi River."

"Wow! The Chicago River has been through a lot," Miguel said.

"About 30 years ago, a magazine article called 'Our Friendless River' told about how badly the Chicago River had been abused," the guide said. "That's when Friends of the Chicago River was organized. We work to make sure the river is useful and beautiful. We want people to enjoy the river, and we want animals, such as that beaver we saw, to thrive in this habitat."

"I didn't know that rivers needed *friends*," Miguel snickered. His mom glared at him. "Uh, I like canoeing and exploring the river," Miguel said.

"What else do you do to be a friend to the Chicago River?" he asked the guide nicely. His mom relaxed her glare.

"We organize volunteers to clean up the river and the green areas around the river by gathering garbage and removing plants that don't belong. We provide educational field trips to let students explore plants and animals in and around the river. We work to persuade politicians to make decisions and policies that help promote a clean and green environment. We also fund projects that help wildlife in and around the river."

"What's your favorite project that Friends has done?" asked Miguel's mom.

"Oh, hands down, the fish hotel is my favorite!" the guide responded.

"There are so many hotels in Chicago, I guess people thought the fish needed one too?" Miguel asked, laughing.

"Fish do like a nice place to rest and eat. The boats and the steep walls around the river make downtown a tough place for fish to survive. They need plants to nibble on and places to hide. The fish hotel is a structure that floats in the river. It's attached to the wall close to the Michigan Avenue Bridge. Plants grow on top to attract insects that fish like to eat. More plants grow below the surface to give the fish places to hide. Then there are four deeper containers for bigger fish to hang out in."

"What kinds of fish *check in* to the hotel?" asked Miguel.

"Fish like the orange-spotted sunfish, blunt-nosed minnows, and black buffalo fish. They all visit the underwater hotel. Largemouth bass come by too.

The plan is to add cameras so people can see all the aquatic life living in the city."

"What a great idea! I really do appreciate all the work you all have done," Miguel's mom told the guide. "This river is so beautiful. I have heard even falcons have made nests in the area again."

"And foxes and minks have returned, along with the beavers," the guide said. "Homes and restaurants are popping up all along the shores of the Chicago River. Leisure activities are growing too. Canoe trips are common, you can take an architectural tour downtown, or go fishing. Friends of the Chicago River has a goal of making nature trails and bike paths along the whole river."

"Oh no way! Our neighborhood has this new trail and a bike path in the park by the river. I didn't know you guys helped put them there. That's awesome!" Miguel said.

"I'm glad you enjoy them," said the guide.

"I'm so glad that restoring nature is important in this city," said Miguel's mom.

"Well, Chicago is now a city that cares about its environment. As with many cities, that wasn't always the case," the guide said.

"Yeah," said Miguel, "it's like people didn't realize they were destroying things back then, so now we have to work hard to fix it."

"So is pollution still a problem today?" asked Miguel's mom.

"It's something we may always have to fight," the guide responded. "The Chicago River still needs friends to help keep it healthy."

"Well, I think this river has two more friends now,"
Miguel's mom said as she winked at Miguel. He grinned.

"All right! Let's move on!" the guide called to the group.
"Maybe we'll spot a fox around this next bend."

"Sweet!" Miguel yelled. "And we get to paddle under
another bridge." Miguel dunked his paddle into the water
and pushed back hard. "I like this river!"

How the Cahuilla Indians Lived in Their Land

BY ANTHONY MADRIGAL

The land of the Cahuilla Indian people lies in the valleys of the San Jacinto and Santa Rosa mountains, and in the foothills and the desert below the mountains in Southern California. The Cahuilla have lived here for many hundreds of years.

The Cahuilla have a close relationship with the natural world around them. They have always believed that the land, mountains, rocks, plants, animals, trees, and hot springs have power of their own and should be treated with the proper respect. They have never thought they had the right to change the land any more than was necessary to live. This belief has led the Cahuilla to create many practices to help them preserve and protect the natural world around them, both in the past and today.

In the past, every Cahuilla person knew stories of how their land came to be. Come Cahuilla elders told the story of Bear, Coyote, and the Three Sisters. In the beginning of time, Coyote became jealous of Bear and the Three Sisters. So Coyote killed Bear and cooked him. Coyote invited the Three Sisters to a meal and served them Bear.

"How the Cahuilla Indians Lived in Their Land" by Anthony Madrigal. From *California Chronicles'* November 1999 issue: "Native Americans of Southern California," © 1999, Cobblestone Publishing, 30 Grove Street, Suite C, Peterborough, NH 03458. All rights reserved. Used by permission of Carus Publishing Company.

The Sisters ate the Bear, but when they found out the evil thing Coyote had done they left earth, taking Bear with them to the sky. We still see all of them as stars in the night sky. Coyote searched and searched for them. One night, he came to a great lake and looked into the water and there he could see a reflection of the Three Sisters. He ran around and round the lake looking for a way to get at the Three Sisters. As he did, he kicked up the earth around the lake and created the mountains of Southern California. In frustration, Coyote dove in after the Three Sisters and drowned. This is just one story about how the mountains around the lakes in the land of the Cahuilla came to be.

The Cahuilla tell many different stories about the origins of their land.

Many Native Americans in Southern California share rich oral stories about land, plants, and animals. The story of Bear, Coyote, and the Three Sisters is one example of a story about the natural world—the mountains, stars, and animals that the Cahuilla knew. The songs and stories of the Native Americans also tell of how people should use the land and other natural things.

In the past, the natural world provided the Cahuilla and other Native Americans in Southern California with everything they needed. Cahuilla people built their homes in small villages located near water sources and food gathering areas. Cahuilla *tingavish* (doctors) and *puvulam* (religious leaders) used some plants as medicines. Hot springs were sources of healing power. Cahuillas often named places in their land by describing natural features, such as "place of acorn trees" or "place of palm trees."

When a plant was eaten, an animal hunted, or something taken from the land, every Cahuilla knew that it must be done in the right way, and that appreciation should be shown.

Plants were very important to the Cahuillas and other Native Americans in Southern California. Those used for food included agave, pinyon, mesquite, and acorn. The most important food for the Cahuilla was *weewish*, a porridge made from acorns taken from oak trees. But plants not only provided the Southern California Indians with food. They also gave the materials needed to make baskets, houses, and other important things. The people believed that plants were placed on earth to serve people, but it was not just a one-way relationship. Plants had to be used correctly. When people collected plants, a part of the plant was usually left behind so it would not die and could grow back. In this way, the Cahuilla used plants for their needs, but still helped to keep the balance of the natural world. The plants were conserved for people and animals to use again and again.

The Cahuilla way of hunting rabbits also shows how Cahuilla traditions helped to conserve their environment. When they hunted, the Cahuilla helped keep the number of rabbits down, so that they would not eat all the plants. At the same time, the Cahuilla did not kill more rabbits than they could use and they did not waste any part of the animal. They ate the meat; used the skin to weave blankets, and even crushed the bones to eat. By hunting some rabbits, the Cahuilla helped to conserve plant life. By hunting only what they needed, the Cahuilla did not endanger the rabbit population.

Today the Cahuilla know that it is more important than ever to protect the land and water. The land is now used by many more people, and in a much greater variety of ways. Although the Cahuilla still live on their land, some of the land today is used to run businesses. There are gas stations, casinos, and sand and gravel operations. The Cahuilla have founded tribal environmental programs, run by Cahuilla people, to protect the land. Some Cahuilla are learning modern ways of managing the environment. They map the land using satellites and computers, and they use modern scientific methods to test for pollution. The Cahuilla believe that these modern techniques cannot do the whole job of protecting the land, though. They still believe they were taught by their stories and songs long ago how to use the land the right way.

Dancing in the Wings

BY DEBBIE ALLEN

My mom calls me Sassy, 'cause I like to put my hands on my hips and 'cause I always have something to say. Well, if you had feet as big as mine, you'd understand why.

I was taller than the rest of the kids at school, even the boys. At our recitals all the other girls got to dance solos and duets, and wear pretty tutus. I was too big for the boys to pick up, and too tall to be in line with the other girls. So I watched from backstage, dancing in the wings, hoping that if I just kept dancing and trying, it would be my turn to dance in the spotlight.

One day at the end of ballet class, Miss Katherine announce, "Mr. Debato from the Russian school is coming next week to look for talented young people for the summer dance festival in Washington, D.C."

The whole room turned into a whirlpool of excitement as the sign-up sheet was posted. Everyone wanted to try, especially me.

But as I wrote my name down, I heard two girls, Molly and Mona, giggle. Mona said, "Oh please, she'll never make it. They said talent, not a tyrannosaurus."

My heart seemed to stand still. For once I had nothing to say.

I couldn't hide the tears I felt welling up in my eyes, so I just grabbed my dance bag and ran to the parking lot.

Late that night I lay awake, staring out my window and thinking. I could see myself dancing on the Milky Way, swirling like a twinkling shooting star. Next thing I knew, I was talking to myself out loud. "I'm goin' to that audition, big feet and all."

And instead of standing in the back, I squeezed between Molly and Mona, right in the front row. I ignored their snickering.

Miss Katherine came in and introduced Mr. Debato. Everyone applauded. Boy was he short! Couldn't have been more than four feet nine inches tall.

He started walking down the rows, pacing back and forth, just looking at us.

The first round of the audition was center floor exercises. Mr. Debato walked around prodding and poking, making corrections. He stopped once and looked right at me but didn't say a thing. I held my breath as he dismissed almost half the kids after the first round. But not me.

Then came the leaps across the floor. I took off like Jackie Joyner-Kersee in the long jump at the Olympics. With one leap I sailed in the air past all the other girls. Molly and Mona watched, lookn' pea green with envy.

When I finished, Mr. Debato yelled, "Young lady, you must learn to dance *to* the music. Up on the count of one, down on the count of three! Three! Not five! You have the rhythm of a troglodyte. Again!"

I was crushed.

By the end of the day there were only seven of us left. Mr. Debato called out everyone's name except mine and asked them to step forward.

Standing alone, I really had to fight to hold back my tears.

Then I heard him say, "Thank you all for coming today. Keep working, keep trying. You are dismissed."

Mr. Debato said to me, "Sassy, you have a great deal of potential. You have beautiful long arms and legs, but you flail about with no control. You must learn to use your feet better—and timing, timing. We have a lot of work to do when you come to Washington this summer. Dismissed." He walked out.

Jumping and shouting, I ran to the parking lot. "I made it! I made it! Mama, I made it!"

One month later Mama and I boarded the plane for Washington, D.C. She held my hand as my heart pounded when we landed.

In class the first day Mr. Debato introduced me to his twelve-year-old protégé, a boy named Dwight who was five feet ten inches tall. "Dwight, I think I have found you a partner. Meet Sassy."

Mama was right— being tall wasn't so bad after all.

By the end of the summer I got to dance a duet with Dwight in the summer concert. When Dwight lifted me high in the air, I felt like I was dancing on the Milky Way.

The Myth of Icarus

Retold by Claire Daniel

Long ago in Greece, there lived a great inventor named Daedalus. The king was unhappy with Daedalus and banished him and his son, Icarus, to the island of Crete. The only escape from this island was by sea. If they tried to use a boat, they would be arrested. The sea was vast and rough, so swimming was impossible as well.

Daedalus thought hard about what to do. Finally, he came up with an incredible idea. If they could not escape by swimming or by boat, then they would fly!

Daedalus spent months designing a set of wings. The wings had to be strong enough to support him and his son on their journey. He collected feathers and sewed them together with string. He held the feathers together on a frame with wax. He added leather straps that would secure the wings on their arms.

Finally, he finished his invention. Daedalus fitted two wings onto his son's strong arms. Then he gave him careful instructions.

He warned, "Icarus, do not fly too low. You must fly high enough so the feathers will not get wet from the sea mist. Damp wings will pull you down, and your arms will tire."

Icarus turned away, ready to fly, but his father stopped him. He added, "Son, do not fly too high either. The heat of the sun will melt the wax, and the wings will not hold together."

And so, Daedalus and Icarus jumped off a cliff, wearing the wings. They flew miles and miles over the sea. They headed towards the mainland, and their wings drifted on air currents. Their arms did not tire.

The flight thrilled young Icarus. He was so ecstatic about his special, new ability that before long, he began ignoring his father's warnings. He soared higher and higher. The soft warm wind blew gently on his face, and the sun warmed his skin. He did not realize that the sun's rays were melting the wax that held his wings together. His wings began to fall apart and Icarus fell into the sea.

The sea swallowed him, and soon after he drowned. Daedalus had lost sight of his son, and reached land alone. Days later, his son's wings washed up on shore. Daedalus figured out what had happened, and he was broken-hearted.

The sea where Icarus died was later named the Icarian Sea. The sea is still named that today, and you can find it off the island of Crete.

Animal Olympics

BY ELIZABETH SCHLEICHERT

Every four years, top athletes compete in the Summer
Olympics. But guess what? In all sorts of sports, animals are
the real winners!

Speedy Swimmers

A *sailfish* is the fastest creature in the seas over short
distances. It can reach speeds of up to 68 miles (109km) per
hour—as fast as cars whizzing along some highways. In fact,
a sailfish makes human swimmers look pathetic. The fastest
Olympic swimmers plug along at only about 5 miles (8km)
an hour.

How does the sailfish do it? It has a streamlined shape, like
a torpedo. It tucks its long "sail" into a slot in its back. And, with
just a few flicks of its stiff, sickle-shaped tail, the fish propels itself
speedily through the water.

High Divers

What bird dives from the greatest height into water? Several
share the honors, including *gannets* and *brown pelicans*.
From 50 feet (15m) or more over the water, these birds plunge
headfirst to catch fish. They have especially strong skulls and
air sacs, which work like air bags, in their breasts. So the birds
aren't hurt when they hit the water. How do humans compare
with these champs? Olympic high-divers drop from a measly
33 feet (10m) above the water.

From "Animal Olympics" by Elizabeth Schleichert. Reprinted from the August 2004
issue of *Ranger Rick*® magazine, with the permission of the publisher, the National
Wildlife Federation®.

Marathon Records

A *gray whale* would win the prize for distance swimming. These fantastic animals swim an amazing 10,000 (16,000km) or more miles a year. They migrate from their breeding grounds off Mexico to their feeding areas off Alaska and Siberia, and then back again.

In the air, the long-distance winner is the *arctic tern*. Many of these birds fly more than 20,000 miles (32,000km) a year. They migrate from the Arctic to Antarctica—and back—catching summertime in both places.

Weightlifting Wonders

Human weightlifters can lift more than three times their body weight while standing in one spot. But *rhinoceros beetles* can lift about 30 times their own weight and walk at a normal pace at the same time! A person with that kind of muscle-power could walk around carrying a pickup truck!

But what about elephants? Surely they're very strong. An Asian elephant, using just its trunk, can lift more total weight than any other creature—a ton or more. But compared to its size, a ton isn't that much—less than half the elephant's weight.

Gymnastic Greats

Lots of animals could be winners in this category! For example, *tree squirrels* are super acrobats. They can leap through the treetops or run along thin branches using their tails to balance them.

Then there are the *gibbons*, small apes in Southeast Asia. They swing by their long arms through the treetops—sometimes letting go and "flying" like a trapeze artist from one branch to another. In one free-form swoop, a gibbon can travel nearly 10 feet (3m).

And don't forget those super show-offs, the *spinner dolphins*. They leap high out of the water and can do four complete spins before flopping back down again. That deserves a gold medal, for sure!

Zoom, Zoom

Cheetahs are super-star sprinters. They can dash as fast as 64 miles (100km) per hour over short distances. How? A cheetah has a super-bendable, spring-like spine. So, with each stride, the animal can gather its legs up tightly, the stretch them w-a-a-a-y out. This helps the animal zoom across the ground.

For high speed over the long haul, the *pronghorn* wins! It can keep running at 35 miles (55km) an hour for many miles. And it can speed up to 50 miles (80km) an hour if it has to.

The fastest humans can keep up a pace of about 13 miles (21km) an hour over many miles. And for short bursts, they can spring as fast as 26 miles (42km) an hour.

So, watch the Summer Olympics. But just don't be too impressed. After all, most of these human competitors just can't measure up to all the winners in the animal kingdom!

Redwoods Are the Tallest Trees in the World

by David A. Adler

The tree near my house is so tall that I can't even reach the lowest branch. The top of the tree is higher than my house. It is the tallest tree on our street. But this summer I saw trees which were much taller. We went to California and I saw the redwoods. They are the tallest trees in the world.

We saw them in a national park in California. The ranger told us that redwoods need a lot of sunlight and water. They grow best where it does not get too hot or too cold, and where there is a lot of moisture in the air. The climate on the northern coast of California and in southern Oregon is just right for the redwoods.

The ranger also told us that redwoods grow about ninety meters high. That's over three hundred feet. The tree near my house is only about fifteen meters, or fifty feet, high.

Redwoods are members of the sequoia family of trees. They are named for Sequoyah, who was a leader of the Cherokee Indians.

Redwoods are evergreens. They have small needles which stay green all year. At the end of the redwood branches there are small round cones. Each cone is about the size of a large grape.

The cone holds about fifty seeds. Each seed can grow into a tall redwood tree, but few of them do. Most young redwoods grow from the roots of other living redwood trees or from the roots of redwoods that were cut down. The old roots take water and minerals from the ground and help the young tree grow quickly.

Many young trees may grow from the roots of just one old tree. We saw redwood trees growing close together in groups. They probably all grew from the roots of the same tree.

New branches grow at the tops of young trees. These new branches and the branches of other trees keep sunlight from reaching the redwood's lower branches. The lower branches die. Some very old redwood trees have no branches at all for the first thirty meters, or about one hundred feet.

It takes about five hundred years for a redwood to grow to its full height. But many redwoods live longer than that. Some redwoods live more than a thousand years. After that the tree begins to die slowly from the top. Sometimes its branches are killed by wind or lightning. Sometimes the tree is weakened by age or fire. Then it is no loner able to send water all the way up to the top branches.

When a tree has been cut down, you can see the rings in the stump. Tree rings tell us how old a tree is. The width of each ring shows how much the tree grew during that year. Sometimes the weather is so bad that a tree grows very little. There is no ring for a whole year. At other times, when the weather is very good, two rings may form in a single year. But years like that are unusual. Almost always the number of rings tells us the age of a tree. And the width of the ring tells us whether the tree grew fast or slow.

The bark of a redwood tree is sometimes almost thirty centimeters thick. That's nearly a foot thick. This thick bark helps a redwood live for such a long time. The roots of a tree collect water and minerals from the ground. The water then travels up the tree trunk to feed the branches and the leaves. It travels through layers just under the bark. The bark protects the layers.

Because the redwood's bark is so thick, it also helps protect the growing part of the tree from fire.

The redwood bark contains tannic acid. This protects the tree from insects and disease.

On the bark of some redwood trees I saw big bumps. The bumps are called "burls." Burls do not harm the tree. They are really redwood buds that did not grow into branches. The burl is hard and beautiful. Some of it is even used to make jewelry.

The wood of a redwood tree is very strong. Things made of it last a long time. Redwood lumber is used to build houses, to make indoor and outdoor furniture, railroad ties, and much more.

Because redwood trees are so tall and straight, there is a lot of valuable wood in each tree. Sometimes there is enough wood in one tree to build four houses.

People are afraid that too many tall redwood trees will be cut down for wood.

To protect these trees the Save-The-Redwoods League buys redwood forests and makes them into parks.

Redwoods are the tallest living things in the whole world. Next to a redwood almost anything looks small. If you ever see one, you will know what I mean.

Catching the Fire

BY MARY E. LYONS

Philip Simmons caught the blacksmith fever when he was thirteen years old. Since then the artist has forged more than five hundred pieces of ornamental wrought iron. Most of his gates, fences, and railings decorate the costal city of Charleston, South Carolina. Several of his finest works are in museums.

To touch a Philip Simmons gate is to touch the past. His craft is over five thousand years old. In 3,500 B.C., Egyptian smiths shaped metal with hammer and fire. In Sierra Leone, West Africa, smiths have worked with brass and copper since the thirteenth century.

From 1670 until 1863, thousands of West Africans were enslaved on the coast of South Carolina. Some were blacksmiths who passed the tradition on to their offspring. One descendant, a former slave, showed Philip Simmons how to work iron.

Like his ancestors, Mr. Simmons can hammer life into a dead lump of iron. But he is the first African American smith known to forge animal figures. His fish and sly-eyed snakes look as lively as he feels. "I like action!" he declares in his musical Low Country speech.

For over eighty years, action has guided Philip Simmon's life and art. Born on June 9, 1912, he claims he retired in 1987. Yet he remains excited about his craft. After a lifetime of seventeen-hour workdays, he still rises at 6 A.M.

Mr. Simmons often wakes with an idea for a new gate. "I see it finished completely in my mind," he says. Before breakfast, he rolls a squeaky chair up to his office desk and sketches the design.

And he will still play "the old blacksmith tune" on his anvil, especially for young people. Youngsters are drawn to his friendly face and teasing ways.

"You are a role model and a mentor," a young fan wrote to him. "You are showing us we can do anything!" said another.

Philip Simmons began his career as an untrained boy. Now he is called the Dean of Blacksmiths by professional smiths across the country. His memories show that skill and patience take years of work. They also prove that everyone can achieve both. An honored artist, teacher, and businessman, Philip Simmons is the working person's hero.

Claudia's Collection

BY ANDREA FITCHA

"Freeze! Don't move," said Claudia.

Her friend Marcus stood perfectly still as Claudia knelt down on the sidewalk in front of him. "What's the matter?" he asked. "I don't have a bug on me, do I?"

"No," said Claudia. "I found a feather. I didn't want you to step on it."

"A feather?" said Marcus. "Big deal. Come on, we're going to be late for school."

It *was* a big deal to Claudia. She was a collector. When she was four years old, her grandpa had given her a tackle box full of fishing lures. She'd loved sorting all the lures by color and shape and putting them into separate compartments. After that, she started collecting all kinds of things. Her room was filled with interesting objects she picked up during the day: rocks, coins, string, even paper clips. She had shells from trips to the beach, leaves and pine cones from the trees in her neighborhood, and leftover beads from her mother's craft projects. Everything she found she put into labeled shoeboxes.

"What are you bringing for Hobby Week?" asked Marcus.

"I don't know," said Claudia, as she picked up a brightly colored rock.

"What do you mean, you don't know?" said Marcus. "Bring one of your collections. You've got a million of them!"

Claudia sighed. She wanted to bring one of her collections, but she couldn't decide which one. The night before, she'd gone through all of her boxes twice. She wanted to bring something really special to Hobby Week.

When they got to school, Mrs. Wilson said, "O.K., who has a hobby to share?"

Claudia kept her hand down. She watched as Katie brought a big box up to the front of the classroom. "This is my money collection," said Katie. "My dad travels all around the world for his job, and he brings me money from the different countries he goes to." She opened the box and took out the coins and paper money. There was money from Canada, Japan, and even Australia! The class looked at all the pictures on the coins. They were surprised that paper money came in so many different colors.

Claudia frowned. She really wanted to be in front of the class, sharing her hobby. But which collection should she bring?

The next day, before school, Claudia looked over the shoeboxes again. Claudia's mother poked her head in the doorway and looked at the rows and rows of shoeboxes that lined Claudia's room. "If this keeps up, we're going to have to move your bed out into the hall," she said, smiling.

"I have plenty of room," Claudia said. "I can stack them all the way to the ceiling if I have to." She noticed she was running late, so she just decided to bring her biggest collection: her rock collection.

At show-and-tell time Claudia raised her hand, but Mrs. Wilson called on Joseph first. He brought a giant wooden case to the front of the class and opened it up.

Claudia groaned. It was the biggest rock collection she'd ever seen! The class oohed and aahed at all the pretty and unusual rocks.

Claudia did not raise her hand again. She hid her shoebox in her backpack until school was over.

The next day, Claudia brought her prettiest collection: her seashells. At show-and-tell time she raised her hand in the air and waved it around, but Mrs. Wilson called on Annie. Claudia watched as she brought up a big piece of poster board. Annie had glued different shells to it and labeled each one. Claudia slid down in her seat and shoved her box of shells under her desk.

The night before the last day of Hobby Week, Claudia emptied her pockets and looked at all the things she had collected that day. She began to sort everything into several different piles. Suddenly, she had an idea. She went into the garage to find her old wagon.

The next day, Marcus brought his telescope and his book about planets. Then Marissa showed the class all the different tricks she could do with her jump rope.

"Does anyone else have something to share?" asked Mrs. Wilson.

Claudia raised her hand. "Go ahead, Claudia," said Mrs. Wilson.

Claudia wheeled her wagon to the front of the class. She brought out all of her shoeboxes and laid them on the table. The class murmured. There were so many boxes they barely fit on the table! Claudia opened each box. Everyone stared at the rocks, seashells, leaves, rubber bands, fishing lure, feathers, and beads.

"Wow! Look at all that stuff!" said Joseph.

"I don't get it," said Annie. "What's your hobby?"

"I collect collections," said Claudia proudly.

Everyone laughed.

"Well," said Mrs. Wilson. "This is definitely the best—and the first—collection of collections I've ever seen!"

One Giant Leap:
The Story of
Neil Armstrong

BY DON BROWN

In 1932, two-year old Neil Armstrong watched airplanes race.

Small, brightly colored planes flashed over Neil and his father, Stephen. The planes raced around a triangle-shaped course, their propellers tearing the sky with a sound that was like an endless thunderclap.

The spectacle surely left its mark on young Neil. Four years later, he leaped at the chance to ride in an airplane.

It wasn't on a racing plane but a three-motored passenger plane nicknamed the Tin Goose. The plane offered rides at the town airport. It could carry about a dozen people.

Neil and his father climbed aboard and buckled themselves into wicker seats. The engines sputtered to life with a terrific noise. The airplane raced down the runway and slowly lifted into the sky.

As the ground dropped farther and farther below them, people, houses, cars, *everything* looked smaller. The Tin Goose plowed through the clouds as gusts of wind bounced it up and down.

The noisy, bumpy ride and ever-titling view worried Stephen Armstrong.

But Neil was fearless.

Neil was delighted.

Neil started making ten-cent airplane models and reading flying magazines.

He also started having a magical dream. In it, he held his breath and hovered above the ground. Below him, people, houses, cars, *everything* looked smaller.

On clear nights, Neil climbed to the roof of his neighbor Jacob Zint's garage. Mr. Zint had a homemade telescope mounted there and welcomed visitors to spy the moon and stars.

Neil looked and looked and looked.

Neil Armstrong earned his student pilot's license on his sixteenth birthday. He was too young to have an automobile driver's license.

In time, Neil Armstrong, student pilot, became Neil Armstrong, navy fighter pilot in the Korean War. Then he was Neil Armstrong, test pilot, flying rocket-powered airplanes to the upper edges of the sky. Eventually he became Neil Armstrong, astronaut.

Astronauts are special pilots who fly spacecraft around Earth. When Neil became an astronaut there was a plan to land people on the moon and then return them safely to Earth. The moon had gripped people's imagination for thousands of years. On July 16, 1969, astronauts Neil Armstrong, Buzz Aldrin, and Mike Collins sat in a cramped capsule atop a Saturn rocket.

At 9:32 A.M. the main rocket motors erupted. Flames spewed from the Saturn's tail as it lifted from the ground. Soon the first set of engines exhausted their fuel and fell toward the ocean. Smaller engines sprang to life and sent the capsule circling the globe.

After two turns around Earth, a final rocket engine blasted the capsule to 25,000 miles an hour and they hurtled to the moon.

When they reached the moon, Neil and Buzz entered a special spacecraft designed to part from the main capsule and land on the moon. Mike remained aboard the main capsule to pilot it as the other two astronauts dropped to the moon's surface.

Earthlings Neil Armstrong and Buzz Aldrin had finally reached the moon!

Wearing space suits and helmets, they opened the hatch of the spacecraft. Before them was the moon, magnificent and empty. Neil climbed down a ladder and hopped to the ground. Special cameras allowed 600 million people on Earth to watch and listen.

"That's one small step for man, one giant leap for mankind," Neil said into his microphone.

Buzz climbed down the ladder and stepped onto the moon's surface.

Neil stood next to Buzz. Their helmets almost touched. Buzz grinned broadly. Neil clasped his hand on his partner's shoulder.

"Isn't it *fun*!" Neil said.

On July 20, 1969, Neil Armstrong stepped on the moon and became a hero to millions of people.

But inside him was the memory of an ordinary boy from Wapakoneta, Ohio.

A boy who loved books and music.

A boy who was shy and made friends carefully.

A boy who dreamed of hanging in the air suspended only by a trapped breath.

Wagons Ho in '44
The Stephens-Townsend-Murphy Party

BY DIANE L. BROOKS

On May 18, 1844, in Council Bluffs, Iowa Territory, forty oxen-drawn, canvas-covered farm wagons assembled. Most were headed for Oregon. But fifty of the people and eleven of the wagons were bound for California, a trip that had not yet been made successfully with covered wagons. The two groups would start out together and then go their separate ways later in the journey.

Half the California-bound company consisted of the family of fifty-eight-year-old Martin Murphy, an Irish Catholic immigrant. Murphy hoped that California's pro-Catholic makeup would allow for a good life for his farming family. John Townsend, a doctor and farmer; his wife, Elizabeth; and her orphaned seventeen-year-old brother, Moses Schallenberger, traveled in one wagon. They looked forward to a better climate and new opportunities. Mountain man Caleb Greenwood had done some exploring and would act as scout and guide for part of the trip. Old Man Hitchcock, who had been a trapper, accompanied his daughter, Elizabeth Patterson, a widow with four small children. Blacksmith Elisha Stephens, a quite but natural leader, was elected captain of the journey.

It took three days to get everyone across the flooded Missouri Rivers. But once the entire party was safely on the other side, the journey across the plains went well. There were plenty of sources of water, wild game for food, and more than enough grass for the animals to eat. The emigrants stopped at Independence Rock in Wyoming for a week to hunt buffalo and rest. Here, the first child to be born on the trail to California arrived. Her parents named her Ellen Independence.

A few days later, Hitchcock suggested that they go directly west instead of heading south and then north on the so-called "safe" trail. After much discussion and a vote, the group agreed. Hitchcock's shortcut turned out to be much longer than originally estimated. But the route (later called Subette's Cutoff), ultimately shaved eighty-five miles off the travelers' trip.

A stop at Fort Hall's trading post in present-day Idaho offered the opportunity to pick up some provisions for the remaining eight hundred miles to California. A few days later, the eleven wagons that were headed for California turned south. Greenwood had not been this far west and could no longer guide, so Stephens followed the rutted trail that the Chiles-Walker party had left the year before.

The journey was monotonous as it followed the more than three-hundred-mile-long Humboldt River. Then, the river abruptly ended at the Humboldt Sink, where important discussions ensued. Should the emigrants journey south, as they believed the Walker party had, or head directly west for a pass through the Sierra Nevada Mountains? Fatefully, the group met a friendly Paiute Indian who described a river about fifty miles away. The emigrants hoped that following the water would show them the way to get through the mountains before the winter snows began.

But first, the pioneers had to cross a long stretch of desert, later named the Forty Mile Desert.

Without Walker's tracks as a guide, the party was on its own. No water would be available along the way, so vessels were filled with water, and food was stored for the animals. After two days of walking, the party came to a river of clear water. The grateful emigrants named it the Truckee River, after the friendly Paiute chief.

The river flowed through a mountain meadow (where Reno, Nevada, is located today), then continued through steep, narrow mountain canyons. In one day, the party crossed the river ten times to travel just one mile along its rocky streambed! Exhaustion began to set in for both humans and oxen. Snow started to fall. Winter had arrived, and with it came more decisions.

The emigrants had been following a river that flowed west to east. But now the river started to flow from the south. Yet, the highest mountains that the party had to cross were west. After a general council, the party decided to split into two. The wagons and most of the people continued west. Two of the older Murphy boys, plus two single men and two women—Elizabeth Townsend and Ellen Murphy—followed the river south on horseback. Their goal was to get to pioneer John Sutter's fort in central California—Sutter's Fort became a stopping place for emigrants on the journey to California—as quickly as possible to inform those inhabitants of the presence of an overland wagon party attempting to cross the Sierra Nevadas.

The wagon group continued west and arrived at the north shore of a beautiful lake (today called Donner Lake). Ahead of the emigrants was a snow-covered mountain wall.

They were not sure where there was a pass through the mountains, if there even was one, or if the wagons could make it. The group agreed to divide again, leaving six wagons with their valuable goods behind for the winter. Schallenberger, Joseph Foster, and Allen Montgomery volunteered to stay and guard the wagons and their contents. The rest of the party shared five wagons on their trip across the mountains.

After searching for days for an opening in the mountains, Stephens finally found one just wide enough for an ox to pass. The oxen were lined up one behind another and led through. Chains were then attached to the wagons. With the oxen pulling from one side and the men pushing from the other, the wagons were lifted over a ten-foot-high rock. But once they were on the other side of the mountain, the snow became chest deep and the oxen could no longer pull the wagons. The emigrants then erected a camp along the Yuba River, where another baby—Elizabeth Yuba Murphy—was born.

Here, another decision was made. The wagons, women, and children (under the charge of two men) remained at the camp. Seventeen men left for Sutter's Fort, which was about fifty miles away, to obtain help and supplies for the rest of the group. The men arrived at the fort a week later to find that the group of six on horseback also was there.

But instead of immediately organizing a relief expedition for those still in the mountains, the men became swept up in the revolution that was brewing against the Mexican government. Following Sutter's lead, they joined the ranks of Californians supporting the Mexican government.

After a few weeks, the Murphys and others decided to turn back and rescue their families.

In February, a rescue party reached the Yuba River camp. Everyone there was still alive, but the food supply was gone. One of the rescuers, Dennis Martin, continued east to locate and rescue Moses Schallenberger, the one person remaining with the six wagons. In July 1845, after the snow had melted, some of the men returned for the wagons.

The Stephens-Townsend-Murphy emigrants proved that people could travel west to California by covered wagon. The group was well organized, selected a good leader, and banded together when decisions were made. No wagons were lost, no deaths occurred, and even two babies were born along the trail. By opening the overland trail to California, the Stephens-Townsend-Murphy group began a new chapter in American history.

There's Something Fishy About This Horse

BY LESLIE DENDY

A sea horse looks like a fairy tale animal made out of a horse's head, a chameleon's tail, and crocodile scales. It's hard to believe a sea horse is really a fish. But if you look closely, every bit of it is fishy. The "strange" arrangements of its fish parts actually help the sea horse succeed in its unique way of life.

About 35 different kinds of sea horses swim in shallow seas around the world. The largest ones would stretch from your fingertips to your elbow. The smallest would fit on a fingernail. A sea horse spends most of its time hiding in a clump of sea grass or coral. It blends in so well that it is almost invisible. When a tiny fish or shrimp comes by— slurp!—the sea horse sucks in the mini-meal.

The "horsey" head with its slim, stretched-out snout is a super-sipper. To create suction, the sea horse moves several bones in its skull, jaw, and throat. Water and food rush in. Lots of other fish suck food in the same way, but the sea horse sucks especially hard and fast because of its narrow snout and tiny mouth. It nabs a tiny fish in less than 1/100 of a second.

The head looks horsey because it bends down. That helps with sudden sucking, too, by providing an element of surprise. The sea horse waits, hardly moving, as a shrimp or fish approaches its head. At the last second the sea horse swings its head up to sucking position. The prey animal doesn't have time to get away.

Head swinging also comes in handy when male sea horses fight each other over females. They actually slug each other with their snouts.

A sea horse has amazing eyes, too. One eye can look forward while the other looks backward, or up, or down. This ability to aim its eyes anywhere lets the sea horse spot animals approaching from every direction while it remains motionless. Like other fish, sea horses never close their eyes, since they have no eyelids.

Of course, this little fish has fins, and it swims with finesse. A sea horse usually swims "standing up"—head up and tail down. It glides slowly forward or backward, up or down, by waving the fin along its back. Two more small fins on the head look like a horse's ears and help steer. Occasionally a sea horse needs to pick up speed, such as when a bigger fish is chasing it. Then it can swim like a regular fish, head in front and tail behind. Sometimes babies also swim that way right after they are born.

Scales are another fishy feature. They are thin pieces of bone that form within the skin. The bony bits in a sea horse's skin grow unusually thick, so they're called plates. They form a stiff coat of armor from head to tail, with protruding knobs and spines. Since a sea horse can't swim really fast, the armor helps protect it from birds, crabs, or larger fish that might try to eat it. If a fish starts to swallow a sea horse, it often spits the prickly thing out.

This body armor also helps a sea horse's tail curl. Instead of waving its tail left and right to swim, a sea horse winds it around a piece of plant or coral. The tail muscles pull on the armor plates, and the plates push the tail into a coil. Sometimes sea horses hang on for hours, waiting for food to swim by. Newborn sea horses will grab anything they touch. They may twist their tails around a grown-up sea horse. Or a bunch of babies may grab on to each other, forming a knot.

After a sea horse hooks onto a "hitching post," it changes color to match its surroundings. That helps it hide both from the tiny animals it eats and from enemies. Sea horses are often brown, gray, or sand-colored to begin with. They can turn red, white, yellow, green, purple, black, or spotted. One scientist watched a sea horse turn bright orange to match the fluorescent tape on her equipment!

Color changing is definitely fishy. Special cells in fish skin contain microscopic specks of paint-like chemicals. Light from the surrounding scenery enters the fish's eyes, and nerves carry messages about the light's color to the skin cells. Then the microscopic specks clump together or spread apart, creating different colors.

To disappear even more completely, the sea horse's skin grows out into whiskery strands, sometimes forming a "mane" on the little horse. To other animals, the strands probably look like seaweed. Sometimes the sea horse lets real seaweed grow on its skin, too.

Sea horses have survived for ages with the help of their snack-trapping heads, their disappearing act, and their twisty tails. People all over the world need to learn more about these fancy fish so we can help them hang on a lot longer.

Dragonfly Wings

BY KEN TAPP

Dragonflies can zoom up to about 30 miles per hour. They can hover in place without going anywhere. They can fly backward for short distances. They can even fly straight up like a helicopter. How do they do it? They have extraordinary wings.

Unlike most other flying insects, dragonflies' two front wings aren't connected to their back wings. This allows the two sets of wings to beat in different directions at the same time to help the dragonflies make exciting twists, turns, and sudden moves. They're so agile that they can catch other insects while they're flying. They especially love to catch and munch on mosquitoes.

To avoid being caught and eaten themselves, some dragonflies use their wings for camouflage. The color spots and vein patterns help them blend into their environment, making it much harder for hungry birds to see them.

Dragonfly wings aren't just useful; they're also quite beautiful. The wings are made of two layers of very thin membranes that are clear or lightly color-tinted and thin enough to see through. Some wings have dark color spots—brown, black, red, or even purple.

Scientists use these color spots and wing tints to help identify the different kinds of dragonflies. For example, the tiny Eastern Amberwing gets its name from the amber color of its wings, and the Twelve-Spotted Skimmer has three dark spots on each of its four wings.

Although dragonfly wings are tissue-paper thin, they're also very strong. The network of veins between the two membrane layers holds the wings together and makes them stiff and tough. These veins carry nerves and hemolymph (insect blood). Along the front edge of each wing, there's an indented intersection of veins called the nodus. The nodus allows the wing to bend and helps with flying. Like the membranes, these veins are sometimes color-tinted. For example, the front edge of a Saffron-Winged Meadowhawk's wing is bright gold—like saffron.

Supported by their stiff wings, some dragonflies are tough enough to withstand long flights. Some Green Darners fly from Florida to the northern United States and Canada to breed. The Vagrant Emperor crosses the Mediterranean Sea, flying from Africa to Europe and Asia. And the Wandering Glider can fly for several days without stopping. Sailors have seen these dragonflies hundreds of miles from land. During their long flights, they feed on aerial plankton, and their wings help them save energy by gliding and drifting on air currents.

Even though dragonflies are expert fliers, their wings can sometimes get them into trouble. If a dragonfly runs into a spider web, its wings can get tangled in the web, leaving the insect helpless. Sometimes a dragonfly will accidentally splash into the water. With its wings spread out and very wet, it's unable to fly and might end up floating until a frog or fish eats it.

When dragonfly eggs hatch, though, the larvae actually live underwater.

When they leave the water to become adults, they pump blood through their veins to unfurl their very shiny wings. As dragonflies get older, the wings lose most of their shine. Once their wings are strong enough, dragonflies fly everywhere they need to go because they can't walk. They use their legs only for holding on to things and for grabbing other insects for dinner.

By the end of the summer, a dragonfly's wings are often tattered and torn. The wings take a beating as the insect zooms around, escaping from birds and chasing other bugs for its next meal. When one male dragonfly comes into another's territory, they often fight each other and hurt their wings. Dragonflies can still fly with damaged wings and even missing a wing, but this makes it harder for them to catch their food. At that point, the dragonfly is near the end of its life.

This summer, if you're lucky enough to have a dragonfly zip close to you or land on you, pay close attention to its amazing wings. It needs those extraordinary wings to catch and eat all those pesky summertime mosquitoes—before the mosquitoes get *you!*

Shobhana's Sari: Coming to Embrace Tradition

BY Tricia Orr

As the auto-rickshaw motored through the dusty street of Sivakasi, Shobhana frowned. Nothing had changed. The sun's rays bounced off the umbrellas the women held over their heads. School children pushed toward home through the stifling heat and red dust.

In bustling Bangalore, the most stylish city in South India, Shobhana had seen girls wearing rough-textured, blue pants called "jeans" and flashy, round earrings as big as field hockey balls.

As she unlatched the gate and entered her home's courtyard, Shobhana's grandmother peeked through the front window's curtain. Shobhana couldn't let her discover the jeans that Lalitha, Shobhana's big-city cousin, had given her before leaving.

A ceiling fan made a rhythmic clicking sound as it rotated lazily, keeping time with Sivakasi's slow, village pace. Shobhana set her suitcases down on the sitting room's red tiled floor.

Her grandmother's eyes shined with relief and excitement. "How was your trip? Are you hungry? Here, let me help you unpack your things. You must be exhausted after the long train ride."

"Shobhana's Sari: Coming to Embrace Tradition" by Tricia Orr, from *Skipping Stones*, Vol. 17, No. 5, Nov. – Dec., 2005. Copyright © 2005 Skipping Stones, Inc. Reprinted with permission of Skipping Stones, Inc.

"It's ok, Achi." But her grandma was already opening the luggage and taking skirts and blouses out and refolding them. Shobhana had hidden the jeans underneath layers of acceptable clothing.

Shobhana tried to get to the jeans first, but then her hand bumped her grandma's. "Oh no, too late," she thought.

Her grandma asked, "What's this?" pulling out the jeans and holding them up as if they were an alien's spacesuit. "Pants for your father? They're much too short for him."

"Lalitha gave them as a gift,"

"A gift for whom?"

Shobhana swallowed hard. "For me, Achi. They're called jeans. Lots of girls wear them in the city."

Her grandma's round face drooped. The smile lines around her mouth sagged. "Why would you want to dress like a boy?"

"Not like a boy, Achi. There's one kind of jeans for girls and a different kind for boys. Can I wear them in the house at least?"

"Shobhana, you're not yet 15, but I want to show you something."

"But what about the jeans?"

Her grandma didn't answer. Instead, she opened a metal cabinet in the bedroom that she and Shobhana shared. "Choose whatever color you like."

When a girl became a young woman she began wearing a sari, a colorful cloth wrapped carefully to make a lovely dress.

Shobhana's heart fluttered at the thought of learning to wear one, while her mind fretted about what would become of the jeans.

"The pink and gold," Shobhana said.

"My, you have a good eye. You chose the pattu sari." A pattu sari was made of the finest silk and worn for special occasions, like The Festival of Lights and for weddings.

Her grandma held the sari at Shobhana's waist. "You see, first you hold a section of it out behind you like this. Then wrap it around you once." Shobhana felt her grandma's warm arms around her.

"Then, fold it back and forth by holding your thumb and index finger as far apart as you can, like this." Shobhana noticed that Achi's fingers, so bent from arthritis, stretch just one inch apart.

"Next, you lay the rest smoothly over your shoulder." As Achi placed the silk over Shobhana's left shoulder, a tendril of hair escaped her chignon and Shobhana glimpsed her grandma's former beauty.

Shobhana felt warm inside, the way she'd felt when her mother, before she died, used to comb her hair while telling her a bedtime story.

She vaguely heard her grandma say, "And finally, you tuck what's left, right in front, like this. There. Now go look at yourself."

Shobhana stepped over to the mirror that hung above their pallets. The gold fabric around the neck of the sari made her brown skin glow like polished bronze. She looked taller, thanks to its elegant drape.

"That's your sari now, Shobhana."

That night, as they prepared for bed, Shobhana tried on the jeans. They felt stiff. The zipper stuck.

She modeled for her grandma, who smiled warmly, "Very . . . modern."

"Girls are crazy about them in the city," she explained.

"I'm sure they are."

Shobhana stripped off the jeans and scooted under the cool, cotton sheet. "I'm really tired from the journey. Good night, Achi."

"Good night, Shobhana," she said, knowing that her granddaughter's real journey had just begun.

Shobhana lay awake in the sultry darkness. She tried imagining herself in the jeans, but her mind returned to the sari. The feeling of silk enfolded her as she drifted off to sleep.

Clothing Around the World

BY MILES HARVEY

China

You may not know it, but you've probably worn things that were invented in China. Do your parents have any clothes or scarves made out of silk? Silk is a very smooth kind of fabric. People in China have been making silk for more than 3,000 years. The silk threads come from the cocoon of a caterpillar called a silkworm.

Do you like wearing sunglasses? The Chinese invented them more than 500 years ago.

India

Do you wear pajamas? The idea for this type of clothing came from India. In fact, the word "pajama" comes from a Hindi word for "pants." These pants look a lot like our pajama bottoms. People in India, however, wear them during the day instead of at night!

Another famous kind of Indian clothing is the sari. Saris are long pieces of cloth, often made out of beautiful fabrics. Women wrap them around their waists and drape them over their shoulders to form a kind of dress.

Do you know what a cummerbund is? It's a kind of cloth worn around the waist. Men often wear cummerbunds with tuxedos.

The idea for the cummerbund comes from India. So does the word itself.

Another kind of clothing that comes from India is the Nehru jacket. It is named after Jawaharlal Nehru, a great Indian political leader. He was famous for wearing this type of jacket.

Japan

The kimono is a kind of robe that people in Japan have been wearing for hundreds of years. Today, the Japanese usually wear kimonos only on special occasions. But in other parts of the world, many people wear gowns or robes inspired by this beautiful type of clothing.

Geta are Japanese sandals made of wood. They are built in a special way to keep your feet well above the dirt and mud!

Russia

Russia gets extremely cold in the winter, so people have to wear very warm clothes. One famous kind of hat that comes from Russia is the shapka. It is made of wool or fur to guard against chilly weather. One well-known type of fur that comes from Russia is called astrakhan. It comes from a kind of lamb.

Another traditional kind of Russian clothing is the valenki boot. These boots are made of felt. They offer great protection against the cold.

The Navajo

Hello, my name is Jill. I am a member of the Navajo (NAH vah hoh) Nation. I live with my family in Window Rock, Arizona. Window Rock is on the Navajo Reservation. The Navajo reservation covers parts of Arizona, New Mexico, and Utah.

The Navajo Reservation is near a part of the United States called the Four Corners. This is where the borders of four states meet. The four states are Utah, Colorado, New Mexico, and Arizona. The Navajo, including my relatives, have lived in this area for hundreds of years.

My state of Arizona is in the Southwest region. I like the Southwest very much because it has many different landforms. You can visit mountains and canyons. Canyons are deep valleys with high, steep sides. Most of the region is dry and hot in the summer. It seldom rains. Many parts of the Southwest have mild winters. The Navajo Reservation is in an area called the Colorado Plateau. A plateau is a high, flat area. The winters there are cold and snowy.

Many of my Navajo ancestors were farmers. They planted crops in low-lying land such as valleys and canyons. These low areas held water from the rain. Canyon walls provided protection from the wind.

My ancestors did not live in a house that looks like the one I live in. They lived in dwellings called hogans. Hogans are one-room houses with as many as eight sides. Some hogans have thick walls. These walls help to keep the inside of the Hogan warm. Some Navajo still live in hogans today.

"The Navajo" from *Scott Foresman Social Studies: Native Americans.*
Copyright © 2005 by Pearson Education, Inc. Reprinted by permission of Pearson Education.

History of the Navajo

The Navajo call themselves Diné (dee NAY), which means "The People." Long ago the Navajo moved from place to place. They hunted and gathered food as they moved. Some historians think that the Navajo originally came to the Southwest from Canada.

The Navajo met a group called the Pueblo (PWEB loh) when they arrived in the area now known as the Four Corners. The Pueblo had lived in this area long before the Navajo arrived. The Pueblo were skilled farmers and builders.

The Navajo liked the Pueblo way of life. They decided to settle near the Pueblo. The Navajo learned how to grow corn, melons, and squash from the Pueblo.

In the 1600s, Spanish settlers brought sheep to the Southwest. The Navajo became expert shepherds, raising large flocks of sheep. The Navajo also received horses, cattle, and goats from the Spanish.

Over time, American settlers began moving to the Southwest. They built farms on Navajo land. Sometimes the settlers and the Navajo did not get along.

In 1864 the United States Army sided with the settlers. Soldiers forced the Navajo to move from Arizona to New Mexico. This trip was called the Long Walk. It was more than 300 miles long. Many Navajo died along the way. In 1868 the United States government decided to allow the Navajo to return home.

Today the Navajo are one of the largest Native American groups in the United States. The Navajo reservation has its own school system and newspapers. It is the largest reservation in the United States.

Government of the Navajo

Long ago the Navajo lived in many small bands. These bands, or groups of families, built their hogans many miles away from other bands. Each band governed itself.

The people in each band also belonged to a clan. A clan is a group of people who are all related. Today there are about 70 to 80 different Navajo clans.

Today the Navajo Nation's system of government is much like the United States government. The Navajo Nation has a president, lawmakers, and other leaders.

Within the Navajo Nation, the reservation is divided into smaller areas called chapters. Each chapter elects its own local leaders. These leaders run schools and organize local festivals.

Other leaders are elected to serve on the Navajo Nation Council. The council creates laws that affect the entire Navajo Nation. The council government meets four times a year in Window Rock.

Economy of the Navajo

Since the 1600s, the Navajo have raised goats, cattle, sheep, and horses. Men used the horses for hunting and to help them keep track of sheep. Young boys and older men looked after the sheep. Sheep were the most important livestock. Many Navajo still herd sheep today.

The Navajo depended on sheep for mutton and wool. They ate mutton, which is the meat from adult sheep. The Navajo fed mutton to visitors to welcome them.

The Navajo wove sheep's wool into blankets and rugs. In the spring, Navajo men cut off the sheep's wool. The women washed, spun, and dyed the wool. Young girls helped their mothers weave the wool. Beautiful, traditional designs were woven into the rugs and blankets. The Navajo people are still known for their weaving.

The Navajo often traded these rugs and blankets with other Native American groups. The Navajo still sell their rugs and blankets to the public. These rugs and blankets are often seen as works of art and are highly prized.

Today the Navajo work at many different jobs. Some have jobs with companies that mine coal or other minerals, such as copper, silver, and zinc. Others work for companies that produce electricity. Still others are doctors, lawyers, teachers, and other professionals. The Navajo Nation runs businesses, such as shopping centers, where many people work.

Culture of the Navajo

The Navajo share many customs and beliefs. Long ago the many Navajo bands gathered to take part in ceremonies for birth, marriages, and deaths. These ceremonies taught the separate bands about the Navajo way of life. Many of these ceremonies still take place in the Navajo community.

Corn has been an important crop since the Navajo began farming. It is used in Navajo ceremonies also. Navajo women often go through a traditional ceremony when they marry. As part of the ceremony, they grind corn for three days. After they finish, they help make a cornmeal cake for the whole community.

A traditional religious ceremony that is still used today is sand painting. The Navajo mix crushed, colored sandstone with charcoal, pollen, and corn dust. This special sand is made in white, blue, yellow, black, and red. The Navajo make large pictures called sand paintings by pouring the colored sand onto a background of smooth, plain sand. The paintings are of important Navajo religious symbols. They are used in ceremonies, especially when people are sick.

All Navajo groups have special songs, called chants, for important events. These chants are still part of the community today. Special people, called chanters, perform these chants. People sing these chants for sick people and for soldiers returning from war. Chants are also used to bless a new home or school or a couple when they marry.

The Navajo share their culture through festivals, such as the Navajo Nation Fair in Window Rock. Visitors eat traditional Navajo foods, such as mutton stew or corn soup. Visitors also listen to Navajo music. They watch artists and craftspeople make rugs and other crafts. The Navajo have held this fair every summer for more than 60 years. It is the largest Native American fair in the United States.

Let's Eat!

BY BEATRICE HOLLYER

Rejoice Thembelihle Mthembu—Thembe for short—is eight years old. She lives with her grandmother, uncle, aunt, and three cousins in the green hills outside the city of Durban on South Africa's east coast. Thembe and her family don't have much money, but they always have plenty to eat because their crops grow easily in the warm, wet climate.

"My favorite food Weetabix, but I don't get to eat it very often. I like to chew on a piece of *umoba* (sugarcane)."

Thembe's village has no electricity or running water. Most days, Thembe walks down to the bottom of the valley where a spring bubbles up through the rock into a pool. She carries the water back up the hill in a clay pot.

Thembe begins her day by helping her grandmother Gogo make a big bowl of *puthu* for breakfast. *Puthu* is a stiff porridge made from maize, which is grown in the fields around the village. Thembe shares the *puthu* with her uncle, aunt, and cousins. Her mother and father live with her father's family in another village. After breakfast Thembe walks across the hills to school.

"When I grow up, I would like a well-paying job so we can spend less time thinking about food."

At school Thembe does some weeding in the vegetable garden. The children either take what they grow home to their families or sell it to raise money for the school. Thembe thinks working in the garden is important but boring—she would rather

Text from "South Africa" from *Let's Eat! What Children Eat Around the World* by Beatrice Hollyer. Copyright © 2003 by Frances Lincoln Limited. Reprinted by permission of Henry Holt and Company.

Read Aloud Anthology

"When I grow up, I would like a well-paying job so we can spend less time thinking about food."

At school Thembe does some weeding in the vegetable garden. The children either take what they grow home to their families or sell it to raise money for the school. Thembe thinks working in the garden is important but boring—she would rather be cooking.

After school Thembe collects some firewood and builds a fire underneath the cooking pot. Sometimes Gogo asks her to climb the lemon or mango tree to pick fruit. Today she needs mealie meal (cornmeal), so she asks Thembe to walk to the grocery store.

On the way home Thembe carries the mealie meal on her head. If she really concentrates, she can do it without holding on. All the women in Thembe's village carry firewood and water this way.

"I like looking at the chips and sweets in the shop. Now and then Gogo has some spare change and lets me buy some."

Thembe starts dinner by boiling the mealie meal to make *puthu*. She knows how to cook most things and only needs help to prepare a whole meal. Tonight's dinner is her favorite: beef grilled above the cooking fire, with barbecued mealies (corn on the cob), *madumbes* (a root vegetable like a potato), *puthu*, and *amasi* (sour milk), which they have as a sauce and as a drink.

The *puthu* is served first to fill them up and make the meat go further. Thembe piles the *puthu* into a bowl with some vegetables and sits down to share it with her cousins. Children, men, and women all eat separately, using their fingers, according to Zulu tradition. As she scoops up the food, Thembe chatters excitedly with her cousins about the big wedding party planned for the next day.

The next morning Thembe helps her aunt Ntombi tie her best skirt and shawl and put on a special headdress for the wedding. Thembe wishes she was going as well, but she has a large family, so her aunt and uncle are going to represent them all.

The bride and groom, who are both related to Thembe, have saved up for a traditional wedding. According to Zulu custom, even if money is short, there must be plenty of food and drink for everyone. Before they leave, the bride's friends pin gifts of money to her headdress. Then they walk in a procession to the groom's village.

When they arrive, the bride's brother dances and sings a story about their family. He acts it out with sticks and shields made from animal skins.

The children at the wedding think the dancing is the most exciting part of the day. Like Thembe, they love dressing up in beaded headbands, belts, and necklaces.

The groom's friends have killed two cows for the wedding feast. The best pieces are barbecued for the men, and the rest is put into big pots to stew. The meat is served with soft, doughy bread, which is steamed on top of the meat in the pots, and lots of different salads.

After a long day of singing and dancing, the guests feast and celebrate late into the night.

Dan Thuy's New Life in America

BY KAREN O'CONNOR

Large grocery stores and shopping malls are familiar sights to most Americans. But to 13-year-old Dan Thuy Huynh (pronounced Dahn Twee Hween), these are among the many surprising aspects of life in the United States. Fast food, movie theaters, computers, and the English language are also new to Dan Thuy and her family since they moved from Vietnam to San Diego, California, after spending three years in Thailand. They have lived in the United States just four months.

Vietnam, Dan Thuy's homeland, is a small country in Southeast Asia about the size of California. It is located south of China between the South China Sea on the east and Laos and Cambodia (also called Kampuchea) to the west.

Dan Thuy and her family are immigrants—people who have moved permanently from one country to another. In some ways, immigrants lead a double life. They are caught between the old culture and the new, between their native language and a new language, between friends in the old place and friends in the new.

When the Huynhs arrived in the United States, they had an advantage that many immigrants do not have.

Several members of their family had come to America during the mid-1970s, so aunts, uncles, cousins, and grandparents were there to greet them.

Many Vietnamese immigrants settle in Southern California because the warm, mild climate is similar to that of their native land. Some choose the area because they know other Vietnamese people there. The sight of people from their homeland helps immigrants feel that they belong.

Many things can slow down the immigration process. When a family like the Huynhs applies to move to the United States, an agent from the U.S. Immigration and Naturalization Service (INS) opens a file of information about the family. The file includes documents such as birth certificates and military records. Sometimes documents must be sent from Vietnam, which can take a long time. The waiting period also depends on the number of people who have applied to immigrate, the number of available immigration officers, and the time it takes to process the applications.

Finally the day arrived when the papers for the Huynh family were ready. An INS agent interviewed them. After they were accepted as refugees, the INS arranged for them to travel to the United States, where their sponsors were waiting.

"We have a proverb in Vietnam," Dan Thuy's father says. "No place is better than my country." I am happy to be here, and I don't worry about anything anymore, but I still have my parents, brothers, and sisters in Vietnam. "I miss them so much."

You Are How You Eat: Chinese Table Manners

BY EUGENE COOPER

Table manners are among the habits the Chinese take most for granted—no grownup needs to be taught these rules. In a Chinese group, the way you handle yourself at the table gives off very clear signals as to what kind of a person you are. Living and doing field research in Hong Kong for five years, I discovered that it was important for me to learn the basic rules of the Chinese table: my wife, a Chinese woman, taught me Chinese table manners as she would teach a child.

At the typical round or square Chinese dining table, each person has a bowl for *fan* (rice or other grain), a pair of chopsticks, a saucer, and a spoon. The *cai* (meat and vegetable) dishes, placed in the middle of the table, are meant to be shared by all. In contrast, each person's bowl is a private object that comes directly in touch with the mouth, while the chopsticks carrying food from the cai dishes to the bowl and mouth connect the personal mouth with the shared table.

With the chopsticks, you take morsels from the shared dishes and place them in your bowl of rice. Then you raise the fan bowl to your mouth and use the chopsticks to push in the food. Letting the fan bowl stand on the table and using the chopsticks to raise lumps of rice from it is considered a sign of dissatisfaction with the food. A guest who eats this way in someone's house insults the host. It also extremely poor manners to suck or bite your chopsticks.

The host usually serves rice from a large pot. When your bowl is filled, you accept it with both hands; accepting rice with one hand suggest disrespect and carelessness. You set down the bowl at your place and wait—it is very impolite to begin eating before everyone at the table has been served with rice. When you finish your rice, you also stop eating the shared cai dishes. To eat cai without rice makes you look like a glutton. Generally, you should stop eating until your host has offered you more rice, or ask politely for more. At banquets diners are expected to fill up on cai, and eating too much rice may be a sign of disrespect for the quality of the cai dishes.

When you have eaten your fill, it's proper to put down your chopsticks. This encourages others still eating to take their time. Upon finishing, you may either remain at the table or leave. A guest of honor is expected to remain until all have finished, however.

No rice should ever be left in your bowl at the end of a meal. Two Chinese authors of a recent report shared this memory: "As children we were always taught to leave not a single grain of fan in our bowl when we finished. Our elders strongly impressed on us that each single grain of rice or corn was obtained through the drops of sweat of the tillers of the soil."

Similarly, you should never put more of any food in your bowl than you can finish. It is also very disrespectful of the meal and the host to leave grains of rice on the table around your bowl. Chinese children often are told that each of these grains will appear as a pockmark on the face of their future wife or husband. Nor do you serve yourself food or tea without first offering to serve your neighbors at table. When tea is poured for you, it is customary in southern China to tap the table with your fingers in thanks.

The most important rule of Chinese table manners is to put others first in everything. Be conscious that you should take a share of all the common dishes, not eat only from those you like best. Children often are told that the best-mannered person eats in a way that does not let fellow diners know which are his or her favorite dishes.

The young should also defer to the old in order of eating: at formal dinners, children may have a separate table. In the household of the boss of the factory where I did my fieldwork, apprentices usually sat with the boss at the family table but were placed at the children's table at the New Year's feast.

At any meal, it is bad manners to take large mouthfuls, to chew noisily, or to eat faster—or slower—than others at the table. In contrast to Western etiquette, most Chinese table setting include toothpicks, and picking your teeth at the table is acceptable, provided you cover your mouth with your other hand.

At a banquet, whole fish, duck, or other items are always served. Including the head and tail is a symbol of completeness and fullness. It is not polite to turn over a fish at the table; when the upper part has been served, the skeleton is lifted off to expose the part under it. Apparently, turning over the fish is taboo among people who work on boats, because the fish symbolizes the boat, and it will capsize in sympathy if a fish is turned over.

Failure by a Chinese person to follow the rules of good manners is regarded with as much distaste as the lapses of manners normally committed by Western visitors to China.

Everybody Cooks Rice

BY NORAH DOOLEY

My stomach was grumbling. Mom was cooking dinner, and I couldn't wait to sit down and eat. "Carrie, will you go out and find Anthony—dinner is almost ready."

Mom is always asking me to look for Anthony. He's my little brother, and he's such a moocher! If he's not playing ball or hopscotch, he's at a neighbor's house tasting their dinner.

I walked outside and looked up and down the street. I couldn't see Anthony anywhere, so I went over to the Diaz's house. The Diaz family lives next door to us.

When I walked into the kitchen, my friend Fendra Diaz and her little brother, Tito, were cooking dinner because their mom was working late. Tito was telling Fendra that she uses too much spice. Fendra said Tito was checking the pot too often, so the rice and pigeon peas would never cook. Their teenage brother, José, told them to pipe down. He wanted to watch TV.

I looked in the pot to see what was cooking. The rice was bright yellow! Fendra told me that her grandmother in Puerto Rico had taught here how to cook with turmeric. Turmeric makes rice yellow. Tito gave me a taste from the cooking spoon. Boy, was it delicious! Then I asked if anyone had seen Anthony. Fendra said Anthony had been there to taste their dinner but had left to help Mrs. Hua and Mei-Li with their groceries. The Huas live on the corner, so I started to walk up the street.

Rajit said his parents were working at their video and gift shop,
so he was bringing them leftovers in a tiffin carrier.

There was a big party at the Krishnamurthys' house last
weekend, so Rajit's mother cooked a fancy, colorful Indian
dish called *biryani*. It's made with peas, cashews, raisins, lots
of spices, and a special kind of rice called basmati rice. I had
tasted *biryani* at Rajit's house the last time I went out looking for
Anthony.

When I told Rajit that I was looking for my brother *again*, he
said Anthony and Mei-Li were blowing bubbles out a window of
the Huas' house.

The Huas came from China a year ago. Mrs. Hua is just
learning how to speak English. We smile at each other a lot.

Mrs. Hua was steaming white rice for her family and the
boarder who lives in the back room. She was also making
tofu and vegetables in the wok—that's a big pan with a round
bottom. Mrs. Hua always makes me sit down and eat something
when I come over.

Everyone at the Huas' house uses chopsticks. Mei-Li, who
is only three and a half years old, can even pick up a single
grain of rice with her chopsticks! Mei-Li laughed at me when
I tried using chopsticks and dropped some vegetables. She
said Anthony was "bye-bye," so I decided to try our backyard
neighbors, the Bleus.

Adeline and Jeanne-Marie Bleu came home for dinner on
their break from their after-school jobs at the grocery store. They
helped themselves to bowls of rice and beans from the pot and
gave some to me. I thought my mouth was on fire! Jeanne-Marie
teased me when I gulped some water.

It was getting late, and I still hadn't found Anthony. Adeline said she had seen him with a kitten in his arms, climbing the fence to our yard. I said thanks and *au revoir*—that means goodbye—and hurried home.

When I walked into the house, Anthony was showing the kitten to our baby sister, Anna. He was explaining to Mom that he was only borrowing the kitten.

Mom was putting our dinner on the table. Her grandmother from northern Italy, taught our grandmother, who taught Mom how to cook *risi e bisi*—rice with green peas. Mom puts butter, grated cheese, and some nutmeg on it. It smelled so good, but my stomach wasn't even grumbling anymore. I told Mom that I was too full to eat. Anthony said that he wanted to eat his dinner, even though he was full, because he loves rice, and that afternoon he found out that *everybody* cooks rice.

Did You Say Toe Food? No, I Said Tofu!

BY DIANE TAYLOR

Haven't you ever heard of tofu? It's a strange food that looks a little like soft, white cheese and has hardly any smell or flavor at all. It was first made by the Chinese over 2,000 years ago and has been enjoyed by people all over the world ever since. Yet, there are still many Americans who have never even heard of it.

So what is tofu? It's also known as bean curd because it's made from soybeans. The beans have to be washed, soaked, ground up, and boiled. What's left after all this *soy milk*. The soy milk must be strained to remove the pulp and then heated again. A *coagulant*, or curdling agent, such as vinegar or lemon juice is added to make it curdle. The curdled milk must be strained once more so that the curds can be separated from the yellow liquid called *whey*. Finally, the curds are wrapped in muslin or cheesecloth and weighted to press out more liquid. Longer pressing makes firmer cakes of tofu.

Of course, the simple way for us to enjoy tofu is to go to the store and buy some. Many grocery stores stock it in the produce section. You'll find it packed in water in little plastic containers.

Although tofu doesn't have much flavor of its own, it easily absorbs flavors from other foods it's cooked with. And strange as it may sound, tofu can be used to make delicious dishes from burgers to brownies.

Tofu is also an incredibly wholesome food. One serving has more protein than a hamburger. And in addition to being loaded with minerals and vitamins, it has absolutely no cholesterol and very little sodium, fat, or calories. It's easy to digest and especially good for people who are allergic to dairy products. Just think, all this nutrition is inexpensive and easy to come by.

Country Kid, City Kid

By Julie Cummins

Ben is a country kid. When he wakes up in the morning, he hears cows mooing and birds singing. Jody is a city kid. When she wakes up in the morning, she hears taxicab horns and fire truck sirens.

Ben lives on a farm, where he and his family raise cattle. From his bedroom window on the second floor, he can see rows and rows of potatoes and beans. Jody lives in an apartment building with her mom and dad. From her bedroom window on the eighth floor, she can see tall skyscrapers and a busy city street filled with cars.

When Ben goes to school, he takes a school bus that drives many miles on country roads to pick up children. When Jody leaves for school, her mom walks with her to the bus stop where a crowded city bus takes her to school.

At Ben's school, when it's time for recess the kids race out to the big field behind the school to play ball. At Jody's school, the playground is surrounded by a high fence that keeps kids from running into the busy, crowded streets after escaping balls.

Ben goes grocery shopping with his mother once a week. They drive up to a large supermarket in the nearest town and fill up two big shopping carts. Jody and her mom walk to the little neighborhood stores every few days to buy fresh vegetables, meat, and bread. They carry the food home in plastic bags.

To see if his grandmother has sent him a birthday card, Ben has to walk out to the road where the mailbox stands. Jody's mailbox is in a large wall unit in the lobby of the building. She needs a key to open it to look for her favorite magazine.

The first snowfall sends Ben scurrying for his sled to go sliding down the big hill with his friends. When it snows in the city, Jody knows to wear boots for walking on the slushy sidewalks. She can't resist jumping in the fresh snow.

At Christmastime, Ben and his dad cut down a pine tree from the woods behind the farm and bring it home on the back of their truck. Jody and her parents buy their Christmas tree from a sidewalk vendor and take it home on top of a taxicab.

When Ben needs to read about a famous person for a book report, his mom drives him to the bookmobile stop. When Jody needs information for a school project, she and her dad visit the neighborhood library.

Every day when Ben gets home from school, his pet collie eagerly greets him and races around while he does his chores. Jody's pet hamster is quiet, sleeps a lot, and exercises on a wheel in a small cage in her bedroom. She feeds him treats and lets him scamper on her bed while she's reading.

When it gets hot in the summer, Ben opens his bedroom window to let in cool breezes. When it gets hot in the summer, Jody and her parents stay inside their air-conditioned apartment with the windows shut. Sometimes they go to an air-conditioned movie.

For summer vacation, Ben is eager to go to Camp Eagle Ridge to canoe, build campfires, and meet new friends. Jody is excited about her first time at Camp Eagle Ridge. She looks forward to swimming, hiking, and learning to ride a horse.

After meeting their counselors and checking out their cabins, Jody and Ben join the other campers in the main hall. Ben and Jody are paired as buddies for a scavenger hunt, and they are very excited when they find a four-leafed clover for their list.

Ben helps Jody climb on and off a horse, and Jody helps Ben braid his lanyard. Both of them have lots of fun swimming in the lake and learning how to paddle a canoe. They win second place in the team canoeing competition.

On the last night of camp, the two new friends sing with the others around the campfire. They promise to keep in touch until they meet at camp again next year. They make plans to send each other e-mails, swap photos of their pets, and share favorite mystery stories.

As soon as Ben returns to his home in the country, he's going to draw a map of the constellations that he can see from his bedroom window to send to Jody. When Jody returns to the city, she is going to send Ben a street map of the city bus routes and mark where her favorite places are.

Country kid, city kid—miles apart but two of a kind.

A Walk in the City

By Lois Lenski

A store is at the corner
    for buying milk and butter,
A woman feeds the pigeons
    with grain in the gutter.

Children in the schoolyard
    swinging happily,
Graceful swooping gulls
    fly in from the sea.

Noises of the traffic,
    whistles and a bell,
Busy Teddy's market
    with its fishy smell.

Alley cats come looking
    for meager scraps to eat,
Man with a burden
    stops to rest his feet.

Poultry market busy,
    cackling hens in coops,
Restaurant at the corner,
    smells of hot rich soups.

The Lois Lenski Covey Foundation, Inc., for "A Walk in the City" from *City Poems*, 1971 Edition, by Lois Lenski. Copyright 1971 by The Lois Lenski Covey Foundation, Inc. Reprinted by permission of licensor.

Sea-going ships at anchor,
  piles of produce hurled,
Soon they will be leaving
  for ports around the world.

A Place Called Prairie

By Rebecca Kai Dotlich

I pedal
through grasses
bone dry, needle-thin,
passing warriors of bitter winds;
blazing star
and prairie rose.

Biking on paths
of powdered rock
I stop, drag my toes
through slow,
   s l o w
      waters
that ribbon, run
ramble along;

from a distance
I watch warm winds
play spring games
   in open yards,
tossing strings
of snow-white sheets
to tumble, flutter, flap
in plum-colored skies—

I breathe in stories
told to me;
when winds came calling,
a fine dust falling
on these same
prairie plains.

A Capital Capitol

BY GINA DEANGELIS

The U.S. Capitol in Washington, D.C., is one of the most recognizable buildings in the world. For more than 200 years, it has been the working site of the U.S. Congress. And over that time, the Capitol has been renovated, reconstructed, and enlarged many times—you could say it has never stopped being built!

In January 1791, French engineer Pierre L'Enfant was asked to design America's grand capital city. L'Enfant submitted his idea to commissioners in August. It included a grand vista about a mile long, at one end of which would be the city's "Congress House." The U.S. government decided to hold a contest to find the best design for the new country's Capitol. The winner of the $500 prize was a physician named William Thornton.

Construction began in 1793, when George Washington used a silver trowel to lay the cornerstone on Jenkins Hill (known today as Capitol Hill). It was hoped that Congress, which had been meeting in Philadelphia, Pennsylvania, could move in by the turn of the century.

By 1796, though, construction already was behind schedule. Worried lawmakers decided to focus on completing the north wing of the Capitol, but parts of that still were unfinished in 1800. Both branches of Congress, the Supreme Court, the District of Columbia courts, and the Library of Congress moved in anyway.

Congress authorized more money for the Capitol in 1803 and appointed architect Benjamin Latrobe to oversee construction. He had the south wing finished by 1811, but by then, the north wing was in need of repair. The War of 1812 (which lasted until 1815) intervened, and Congress refused to worry about the building project. A frustrated Latrobe resigned in 1813.

In August 1814, an invading British force set fire to the Capitol, the White House, and other government buildings. A timely rainstorm saved the burning city from complete destruction, but Congress was forced to meet for a time in a cramped hotel. From 1815 to 1819, the Senate and the House gathered in a brick structure where the Supreme Court building stands today.

Congress begged the efficient Latrobe to return, which he did, until he resigned again in 1817. His replacement, Charles Bulfinch, designed a beautiful copper-covered dome for the central section of the Capitol. The building finally was completed in 1826, more than 30 years after construction began. The project cost $2.5 million, a staggering amount for the time. And of course by then the United States had grown, so Congress again needed more space.

Another competition to expand the Capitol in 1850 resulted in a five-way tie. President Millard Fillmore chose Thomas U. Walter to supervise construction. Bulfinch's dome was dwarfed by the enormous new wings, so Walter came up with a design for a huge dome and displayed a drawing of it in his office.

Congressmen who visited there were so impressed that in 1855, they voted to replace the original dome with Walter's grand design.

Though the outbreak of the Civil War (1861–1865) briefly interrupted construction, President Abraham Lincoln refused to stop the project and was inaugurated in 1861 beneath the half-completed dome. In December 1863, the final section of the 19-foot-tall Statue of Freedom was hoisted into place. Three years later, the building, with its great domed Rotunda that is so recognizable today, was completed.

The Capitol, however, still required renovation and repair. For example, the decade between 1890 and 1900 saw the installation of electric lighting and modern plumbing. And, all the enlargements made in the first 100 years of the building's life did not ease the eventual overcrowding. Instead of adding more onto the Capitol building, though, government offices and departments moved out. In 1897, The Library of Congress went into the first of three buildings it would use. In 1908 and 1909, two new structures with office space for the House and Senate, respectively, were ready for occupation. The Supreme Court moved into its own building in 1935.

With even more structures acquired, built, and added between the 1950s and 1990s, today that area of Washington, D.C., is called the Capitol Complex. And renovations to the Capitol building are ongoing.

An upgrade of the fire alarm and sprinkler systems, as well as the construction of a new underground visitor center, are being completed.

The Framers of the Constitution considered Congress to the most important branch of the federal government, and the Capitol, the headquarters of Congress, is an impressive symbol of our government.

Miss Liberty Takes Her Stand

BY LYNN RYMARZ

By January of 1885, French sculptor Frédéric-Auguste Bartholdi had begun carefully dismantling his colossal masterpiece, *Liberty Enlightening the World*. The statue had taken him fourteen years to create. With the help of French craftsmen, Liberty had gradually emerged till at last she towered high above the Paris rooftops. She stood 151 feet tall from the base of her feet to the top of her torch.

His "daughter," as Bartholdi called her, had been built as a gift from the people of France to the people of America. It commemorated over one hundred years of friendship since the French had helped America gain her independence from England.

Bartholdi dreamed of one day seeing his statue on Bedloe's Island in New York harbor, standing proudly as a symbol of friendship and freedom. But as the pieces of the statue were packed into 214 wooden crates for the long ocean voyage, he worried. Miss Liberty had nothing to stand on. The American Committee, which had agreed to raise the money for the statue's pedestal, could not come up with the remaining funds to complete it.

The committee had raised half of the money for the pedestal, but nearly all the contributions had been given by the people of New York City.

Many Americans at the time believed it was New York's statue; therefore, New York should pay for it. Others felt that the French should pay for the pedestal, since the statue was from them.

Still, with half of the money raised, work on the pedestal's foundation began. Unfortunately, it did not take long for the committee to run out of money, and work on the pedestal ground to a halt. They needed $100,000 to complete it, but the committee members didn't know where to turn for help. They finally appealed to Grover Cleveland, the governor of New York. When he refused to dip into state funds, the committee asked Congress. But Congress also said no.

The committee's efforts had failed, and funding for the pedestal looked hopeless. The members printed a letter in the paper stating, "If the money is not now forthcoming the statue must return to its donors, to the everlasting disgrace of the American people, or it must go to some other city, to the everlasting dishonor of New York."

It appeared that Frédéric-Auguste Bartholdi would never see his dream of the Statue of Liberty standing on American soil fulfilled.

Then one day Joseph Pulitzer, publisher and editor of the New York *World* newspaper, stepped forward. Having heard of the committee's struggle to come up with the money, he offered his help. "Of course you know that I will do everything I can do to finish the pedestal," he wrote to the American Committee.

Joseph Pulitzer knew that the people of France had raised the money for the statue—laborers, tradespeople, shopgirls, and artisans.

Likewise, he wished to appeal to Americans to do the same. He needed to convince them that the statue was meant as a gift to all the people of America, not just the people of New York.

And so on 16 March 1885, Pulitzer printed an editorial in his newspaper stating, "Money must be raised to complete the pedestal of the Bartholdi statue. It would be an irrevocable disgrace to New York City and the American Republic to have France send us this splendid gift without having provided even so much as a landing place for it. . . . Give something, however little,. . . . Let us hear from the people."

And the American people responded!

As pennies, nickels, dimes, and dollars flowed in the *World* office, Joseph Pulitzer printed each and every one of the donors' names and messages in his paper.

Two little boys contributing to the pedestal fund wrote, "Please receive one dollar for the pedestal. It is our savings. We give it freely." A poor office boy sent money to the paper, writing, "Inclosed please find five cents toward the pedestal fund. As being loyal to the Stars and Stripes, I thought even five cents would be acceptable." A young girl heard about the pedestal fund and wrote, "I am ever so glad I was born in time to contribute my mite to the pedestal fund. When I am old enough, I will ask my papa and mamma to take me to see the statue, and I will always be proud that I began my career by sending you $1 to aid in so good a cause."

During the following month, contributions rolled in. Like the people of France who had contributed to the statue, Americans across the country—from schoolchildren and the elderly to newly-arrived immigrants and working people—had dipped into their pockets to contribute toward the pedestal.

On 11 August 1885, the headline of the *World* read, "ONE HUNDRED THOUSAND DOLLARS! triumphant completion of the *world's* fund for the liberty pedestal."

Work on the pedestal resumed as stonemasons began setting granite stone and mortar into place. Through the fall, the winter, and into the spring, workmen continued building while the pieces of Liberty remained in their wooden crates, waiting for the pedestal to be finished.

By April of 1886, the last stone of the colossal pedestal was about to be put into place. But before they set it, the joyous stonemasons took pennies, nickels, and dimes from their pockets and sprinkled the coins into the mortar. The pedestal would be a lasting tribute to the American people who had reached into their own pockets for the funds to complete it.

Liberty was now ready to be reassembled. Workmen hoisted beams one by one onto the pedestal, then carefully emptied Liberty's pieces from the crates and riveted them onto the steel skeleton. They bolted 600,000 rivets to hold Liberty's 300 copper-skin plates in place.

Slowly she began to take shape: her feet, her gown, her tablet, her face, her crown, and finally, her torch—to enlighten the world.

At last she was completed!

On 28 October 1886, Frédéric-Auguste Bartholdi arrived
for the unveiling and dedication of his Statue of Liberty.
Thousands of admirers cheered and applauded at seeing
the statue's magnificent presence proudly looking over
New York harbor.

None was prouder than the creator himself. "It is as I
wished," he said. "The dream of my life is accomplished."

Miss Liberty still stands today as a symbol of friendship
and freedom, just as Frédéric-Auguste Bartholdi had
dreamed she would.

Elsa

BY JOY ADAMSON

The true story of a lioness who was brought up from cubhood by Joy Adamson and her husband, a senior game warden; they taught her to stalk and kill for herself so that she could be set free into the African Jungle. Elsa's sisters were sent to the Rotterdam Zoo, but Elsa and the Adamsons had grown quite found of each other. Here's how Elsa finally learned how to be free.

Elsa began to show an increasing interest in going off on her own. She was nearly two years old and her voice was getting much deeper. Often she stayed away from two or three days and we knew that she several times joined up with other lions. But she was as affectionate as ever when she saw us again.

We now began to wonder whether we could release Elsa back to the wild instead of sending her to join with her sisters, as we had originally intended. It would be an experiment worth trying, and we thought we would take her to a place where there was plenty of game, spend two or three weeks with her, and if all went well leave her.

Elsa traveled in the back of my truck and the morning after our arrival we took off her collar to show her that she was free. She hopped onto the roof of the truck and we set off to explore the territory.

Up to now we had always given her her meat cut up. Although she knew how to retrieve we were not sure whether she knew how to cope with a dead animal, but if she was to be left alone, she would have to learn.

To our surprise and delight we discovered that even though she had had no mother to teach her she knew exactly what part of an animal was eatable and what should be buried. But she had no idea how to kill. However, we left her where there was plenty of game, hoping that hunger would force her to attack.

But she hated being left on her own and when we went to see her she was terribly hungry and had obviously not eaten since our last visit. After we had given her a meal she fell sound asleep.

We decided to move her to a climate which would suit her better. The new home we chose for her was only some twenty miles from her birthplace. It was really a beautiful place with a river running through it where many wild animals came to drink.

We stayed with her for several months while she learned all the things her mother would have taught her. One afternoon she refused to go for a walk with us and disappeared until the next morning. We realized she had made friends with a wild lion and that the time had now come.

We therefore drove to another river ten miles away where we planned to spend a week before returning to see how she had managed without us. Although I knew it was for her good, I could not help feeling we were deserting her.

At last the week of waiting ended. On our return we fired a shot and Elsa came running out of the bush, overjoyed to see us. She was thin but not hungry, for she showed no interest in the buck we had brought her.

After this we paid her short visits at frequent intervals, and although she was always delighted to see us it was quite obvious that she could manage without us.

I went to England for a long time that summer, and after my return she was particularly pleased to see me.

We had always hoped that she would find a mate and that one day she would walk into our camp followed by a family.

You can imagine our great joy when a few months later she swam across the river followed by three fine cubs.

A Little Freedom

BY WALTER KIRK

"Push me harder, JAK! I want to swing higher!" Billy Norton cried as he whizzed through the air on his swing.

"Me too, JIL," echoed his sister Laury, whistling through the air on the swing next to him. She pumped her legs back and forth, trying by herself to increase her speed. "Whe-e-ee!" she let out a long exclamation of joy.

"Come on, JAK, push me so I go as high as the house roof," continued Billy.

"Now, Master Billy, you know I can't," answered X-2196JAK7 (JAK for short). He continued to push Billy on his swing with exactly the same amount of force he had been using.

"You're my robot," returned Billy. "You're supposed to do everything I tell you to."

"Master Billy, you know very well that's true only up to a point," put in X-2196JIL8 (JIL for short). "We're not allowed to do—or to let you do—anything that would put you in physical danger."

"Such as yesterday," added JAK, "when you were just about to run out into the street after that beach ball."

"There wasn't any traffic," objected Billy.

"That's not the point," continued JAK. "There might have been. Did you stop to look left and right and then left again before you headed into the street?"

"Well—no," admitted Billy.

"There. That's why I grabbed you and pulled you back."

"But did you have to grab so hard? I've got a bruise on my arm there. See?" Billy let go of one of the chain supports of the swing so that he could point to his upper arm.

"Don't!" said JAK sharply.

"And that's why we won't push you harder or let you swing higher," said JIL. "Anyway, there are times I suspect you do things just to tease us."

"Uh-oh, Billy, they're on to us," laughed Laury. "All right, JIL, that's enough. I'll stop now."

JIL stopped pushing and stepped back, letting the swing move through smaller and smaller arcs until it finally came to a standstill. Laury jumped off. "I'm tired of swinging, Billy. Let's go in."

"Okay. Stop, JAK," answered Billy. He, too, slowed down and got off the swing.

"You know what else?" continued Laury with a frown. "I'm tired of these swings, and I'm tired of this slide and this teeter-totter, and I'm tired of this backyard. I'd like to go to a really big amusement park, like Roswell Gardens."

"Yeah, well, Mom and Dad said they'd take us there when we get older," answered Billy.

"I'm also tired of waiting," returned his sister. "Even if we could go to Riverside Park. They've got that slide there that's taller than our house."

JIL and JAK were following Laury and Billy into the house. Now JAK said, "You two have your birthdays in two weeks and three days. You'll be ten years old. Maybe your parents will let you do something special for your birthday."

Billy and Laury's birthdays were on the same day because they were twins.

Their parents, Mr. and Mrs. Norton, didn't believe that twins always have to dress alike and do everything else alike. They encouraged their children to dress and act differently, to be individuals. Still, it was funny how many of the choices Laury and Billy made were similar. They didn't own any matching shirts, but even their parents had to laugh on the many times when Billy and Laury, dressing separately, both chose, for example, red.

Now they were going on ten, and for all of these ten years the twins had been attended to, guarded by, played with, and—yes, nagged at—by the robots X-2196JAK7 (JAK for short) and X-2196JIL8 (JIL for short). The robots also looked a lot alike, but then, robots do. They weren't twins, though. They were two out of 784 that had come out of the factory on the same day. Although they had been special-ordered by Mr. and Mrs. Norton to care for what they were sure would be very special children.

And so Laury and Billy had grown up with JIL and JAK, had spent most of their time with them, and were really quite fond of them. Even if the humans did sometimes get tired of the robots' ceaseless fussing over them.

Now JIL answered Laury's comment. "You know very well why your parents won't let you go to Riverside Park. The last time we took you there, you *ditched* us! We spent an hour and a half wandering through that park, calling your names, while you took a duck boat out on the river."

"You got us into a lot of trouble with your parents for that little escapade," added JAK.

"And we—and they—aren't likely to let that happen again!"

"Well," answered Billy, "we're sorry we got you into trouble. We won't anymore.

Still," he added as he and Laury went in the house, followed by their always companions, "a little freedom would be nice."

A week went by. Then one evening JAK and JIL came into the kitchen where Mr. Norton was sitting with Laury and Billy. They were discussing what the kids might work on for a science project while Mrs. Norton finished cooking dinner.

"Yes, JIL, JAK?" said Mr. Norton after he noticed the robots had been standing there, respectfully quiet, for several minutes. "Do you want something?"

JAK and JIL looked at each other. "You," JIL said.

JAK took one step forward. To Mr. Norton, it seemed as though he were clearing his throat—if robots cleared their throats. "Dear Norton family," he began. He stopped and looked round at JIL, who nodded at him. He continued, "We would like our freedom."

"Your freedom?" echoed Mr. Norton. "You mean, you don't want to work for us anymore? You mean, you want, you want—"

"To be free, yes." finished JAK.

"No-o-o-oo!" Billy and Laury wailed simultaneously.

Mrs. Norton turned a burner on the stove to LOW and joined the conversation. "But why?" she asked. "Don't you like us?"

"You're fine," answered JIL, who apparently couldn't resist joining in herself. "You've been very good employers."

"And of course we love Laury and Billy—" continued JAK.

"As much as robots can love," finished JIL.

"Well, then?" asked Mr. Norton.

JAK began, "Seven days ago, Billy mentioned freedom and how nice it is. And we've heard about freedom and read about it for years—"

JIL added, "Freedom of the press, freedom from slavery, religious freedom, freedom from underarm embarrassment—"

" 'The land of the free, and the home of the brave.' It sounds like a nice thing, freedom," finished JAK.

"It is, it is," said Mrs. Norton thoughtfully. "It's more than nice—"

"It's terribly important—to us humans," added Mr. Norton.

Billy said, "Our teacher Ms. Clive says our freedom is as important as the air we breathe."

Laury said, "But you can't be free—you're robots. And besides, we need you!"

"You're growing up, now," said JIL. "We're probably going to be too small for you in a year or so."

"And we know that we're outmoded now, technologically," added JAK.

"That's true," said Mr. Norton. "There have been at least a dozen new models since we got you. But you know, we could update your circuitry, get you polished up some—"

"We thank you for the offer," said JAK, "but we've served you loyally for ten years, almost, and we'd like to be free now."

Mrs. Norton looked back and forth between Billy and Laury and JIL and JAK. "Really," she said hesitatingly, "you belong to the children."

Laury and Billy seemed almost on the verge of tears.

"But—but—" began Billy.

"We'd miss you!" Laury burst out.

Another week went by. Laury and Billy found their parents watching the news on television.

"Mom, Dad," Billy said, "we've been thinking a lot."

"Yes, a lot," put in Laury.

"And?" prompted their father.

"And, well, we're going to have our birthday in three days—"

"You'll be ten years old," interrupted their mother. "Think of that!"

"Uh-huh," Laury picked up the thread. "Well, you know how some people *get* presents for their birthdays, and some people *give* them?"

"Yes?"

"See, we know we're going to get lots of stuff," Billy continued, "from you and Grandma and Grandpa and Aunt Evelyn and Uncle George and Aunt Connie and everybody—well, we'd like to give something too."

"I think that's perfectly sweet," commented Mrs. Norton. "What did you have in mind, darling?"

Laury said, "See, we thought a lot about this—"

"I said that already!" Billy hissed at her.

"Yes!" Laury returned. Then she faced her parents and said, "JAK and JIL. We'd like to give them their freedom."

They all talked for some time. Mr. and Mrs. Norton pointed out that the kids didn't have to do any such thing, that the robots were theirs for as long as they wanted them. But Billy and Laury kept insisting, because after all, the robots had *asked* for their freedom very nicely. "And besides," Billy concluded, "They deserve it."

Mr. and Mrs. Norton couldn't argue with that, and so they agreed that on Laury and Billy's tenth birthday they could give JIL and JAK their freedom.

"But you know what?" Billy said to Laury when they were back in their room, "They won't be the only ones getting a little freedom!"

Three days went by. The good-bye wasn't an emotional scene, exactly—robots don't cry, and Laury and Billy had determined that they *wouldn't* cry, so that nobody would feel bad. It was rather solemn, in fact, more like a graduation ceremony. But finally JAK and JIL—after saying "Thank you, and happy birthday!"—were headed down the sidewalk and down the street and out of sight.

Four hours went by. The doorbell rang. Billy answered it, his arm bandaged up from wrist to elbow. There stood JIL and JAK. "Uh—hello," said Billy.

"Whatever did you do to your arm?" demanded JIL.

"Oh, well, I—uh—I was playing in the swing, and I went too high, and I fell out. Yeah, I know I should have listened to you!" he added before the robots could scold him any further. "Anyway, the doctor says it's not broken, it's just a bad sprain."

"But you—" said Laury, who had appeared right behind Billy. "What are you doing here?"

"Well, you see," began JAK, "you gave us our freedom—"

"What's the matter? Don't you like it?"

"Oh, we like it fine," picked up JIL. "But you forgot to tell us—"

"What?" prompted Billy.

"You forgot to tell us—what we should do now."

The Guitar Lesson

BY BRETT PACER

Cal Whitlaw slipped his backpack off and held it by its strap as he leaned close to peer at the names over the mailboxes. There it was: *Ray Sacher, Guitar Studies, 2B.* Feeling a mix of anticipation and dread, he opened the heavy glass door and started up the long flight of stairs. The stairway was roomy, but a little dingy, and some of the stairs let out protesting squeaks when he stepped on them. *You'd never be able to sneak up on somebody in this building*, Cal thought as he labored up the seemingly endless flight.

"No!" his father had declared last week when he had asked his parents to buy him a guitar. "You don't have a particularly good record when it comes to following through on things."

Cal braced himself for the lecture he knew would follow.

"Remember those fish. . ." his father had started.

Cal cringed, remembering the goldfish he had probably let die because he hadn't bothered to change their water—and after promising that if he could have the fish he would certainly take care of them.

"Tell you what, though," his father had continued. "I'll rent you a guitar, but only if you'll take music lessons—and only if you practice."

"I will. I promise," Cal had replied.

Cal's mother had touched his father's arm. "There's Ray," she had suggested.

"You're right. Yes, good," he had returned. "Cal, you know your Uncle Ray teaches guitar now. He's got a studio down on Brown Street. I could give him a call, see if he's willing to take you."

That's how it had been arranged, and today was Cal's first lesson.

Uncle Ray. Cal didn't remember the man, really. He and Aunt Julie, Dad's sister, had been living in another state but had just moved back into town last year. Since then Julie had visited the Whitlaws, but Ray had been busy with something or other. Cal hadn't remembered Aunt Julie, either. But then, he hadn't seen her since he was two or three years old. She had been nice, though, very friendly, but she didn't push. She hadn't insisted on hugging him and smothering him with kisses just because they were related. And she was funny, Cal recalled. Yes, he liked that.

But what would Uncle Ray be like? Cal would find out soon enough, because here was the door marked 2B, a wooden door with a translucent glass inset. Cal gathered his courage and knocked.

"Come on in," a voice answered, and so Cal turned the handle and opened the door.

The studio was surprisingly large, maybe a little larger than a school classroom, and with a very high ceiling. And it wasn't at all dingy; a fresh coat of pale yellow paint made it cheerful, even. And bright, because one whole wall was windows.

And striding across the studio with hand outstretched was Uncle Ray.

He was not as tall as Cal's father, but he was lean and wiry, and his thinning hair was long and caught in back in a ponytail. Cal had never seen a man in a ponytail before, not in person.

"Cal?" Uncle Ray said, smiling. Cal nodded nervously and shook the hand he was offered. "You probably don't remember me," the man chuckled sympathetically. "You were too young when your Aunt Julie and I moved away. Put your stuff over here, and come and sit down." Cal dropped his backpack where his uncle indicated and went to take a wooden chair beside an old desk that was heaped with papers and catalogues and books of music, with a wooden guitar perched on top of it all. Uncle Ray took a wooden swivel chair and leaned back comfortably.

"So," he continued, still smiling, "you want to learn guitar."

"Yes, please," Cal managed to gasp out. Where had *that* come from?

"What I'm here for. But first I want you to take a look around. All these guitars? Tell me which one you like the most."

Cal looked at his surroundings. There were a few posters and a cluster of framed photographs, plus a dozen or so guitars mounted on the walls. He was immediately drawn to a red one hanging opposite. He pointed. "That one," he said.

In response, Uncle Ray got up and lifted the guitar down from the wall. He carried it horizontally in his upturned palms and handed it that way to Cal. It was surprisingly heavy. Cal let it rest in his lap as he studied it.

It was a bright cherry color, with a sunburst on top that shaded from light to dark. It had shiny chrome fittings, and it was polished so brightly it seemed to gleam from within. *It's really beautiful!* Cal thought. He was tempted to pluck a string, but he didn't dare.

"Now that you've got that," Uncle Ray said, resuming his seat, "what are you going to do with it?"

Cal was startled by the question. "Uh—" he hesitated, "play my music?"

"And what music is that?"

"You know—music. Like on the radio, in the videos, like that."

"Oh, you mean—" Uncle Ray paused to pick up the guitar from the desktop. He started strumming and belting out made-up lyrics. "Oh-h-h, oh-h-h, baby, baby, baby, baby!"

Cal was just puzzled now. Was Uncle Ray serious, or was he making fun of him? "Well, uh—yeah, I guess," he mumbled.

Uncle Ray put down his instrument, rose, and lifted the cherry-colored guitar from Cal's lap. He held it, as before, in two hands, almost reverently. "Cal, my man," he said, serious now, "using this guitar to play that kind of music is like-like a having a sports car that you only drive to the corner convenience store. It's like having a soul filled with poetry, but you only write 'Roses are red; violets are blue.' Am I making any sense here?"

Cal felt his face flush because he really didn't get what his uncle was driving at. He wanted to say, "No," but he thought that might spoil his chance.

Instead, he ventured, "You mean—you don't like rock music?"

"No, that's not what I mean. Not what I mean at all," Uncle Ray answered. He went to hang the red guitar back in its place on the wall. "Rock? Hey, I grew up on the stuff. What do you think we were playing when we were on tour?" He gestured toward a large framed poster that showed a guitar sprouting wings. Bands of bright colors danced in the background and then somehow managed to swirl themselves into spelling out *Mockingbird*. Cal got up to look at it more closely.

"Is that you?" he asked.

"For twelve years, it was," Uncle Ray answered.

"What happened?"

"Oh, some of us got too old to tour all the time. Some of us wanted to settle down. Me, I wanted to try something else, explore new forms of musical expression."

Cal was beginning to feel a little more at ease with his uncle by now. "Means of expression? What do you mean?" he asked.

"I don't think I'm explaining myself very well," his uncle answered. "Look, there's nothing wrong with rock. There's nothing wrong with any one category of music. But if that's all you can play . . . ." Back at his desk, Uncle Ray picked up the old wooden guitar and sat. Cal sat back down too. "Here, let me show you . . . ."

Uncle Ray started playing then. It was a simple melody, played one note at a time. Cal almost laughed aloud when he recognized the old nursery song "Twinkle, Twinkle, Little Star." "Okay, I know what that is," he started to say.

But Uncle Ray just smiled at him. "Wait," he mouthed. Suddenly he took off, playing, playing, playing.

But it was no longer "Twinkle, Twinkle, Little Star"—or was it? Cal thought he heard the tune again, then lost it, then found it again. Gosh, that almost sounded like the melody upside down. Was that even possible?

Ray Sacher's face twisted with emotion. His fingers were a blur as they flew over the strings. Chords and crests and waves of music filled the room, now fast, now slow, now happy, now sad, now-making you want to get up and dance. Cal did, in fact, find his toes tapping at one point.

The music stopped before Cal realized it. "That was the Hungarian composer Dohnányi," [doh NAHN yee] Uncle Ray announced quietly. "This is Sacher."

Suddenly he was off again. Now he managed to make the guitar sound like an organ, grand and swelling, but somehow that changed into something swingier, and then *that* changed into a series of amazing jazz riffs that left Cal breathless. Then he heard the simple nursery rhyme melody again, and then it was over.

Cal sat stunned. He had never heard guitar music like that before. He wouldn't have thought it possible to get so much—well, so much *music*—out of such a simple instrument.

"Wow!" he said.

"See, Cal," Uncle Ray resumed, "if I teach you some chords, say, A, D, E minor—" he demonstrated each chord as he named it "—you can put them together and play a rock song. Or lots of other kinds of music, for that matter. But if I teach you a larger musical vocabulary—"

and here he performed an intricate little exercise that
Cal did not recognize "—there's just no end to what you
can do."

"You mean—I could learn to play like that?"

"Sure. It's not easy. And I've had years of practice, don't
forget. But you've got to want to do it."

"Yeah, I do—"

"And you've *got* to practice."

"Oh. Well, sure."

Uncle Ray laughed. "I understand. You don't have to
commit to anything right away. There's time. Tell you
what," he added, leaning forward. "I will teach you—"
here he struck the same three chords again, but without
naming them "—and show you how they fit into songs.
That way you can have some sense of accomplishment
right away. Then we'll go back to learn the single notes
and how they fit together. And then-well, we'll see what
happens. Fair enough?"

Cal grinned back at his uncle. "Fair enough."

"I'll call your dad tonight," the man continued, "and
find out how much he wants to spend on the rental. I
might even have a guitar here that you could use. If not,
I'll go with you to pick one out. Then we can have our first
real lesson next week."

"Cool!" Cal replied.

"And welcome, my nephew," Uncle Ray grinned, "to the
World of Music!"

As Cal headed back down that long flight of stairs,
he realized that "Twinkle, Twinkle, Little Star" was back,
replaying in his head. He remembered the thrill he had
had hearing its variations and couldn't wait to start
working on a variation of his own.

Toothpicks, Bottles, Tin, and Rocks

Whenever Wayne Kusy sees a tiny toothpick, he thinks of a huge ocean-going ship. To Wayne, a toothpick is not just a sliver of wood. It's a way for him to express his creative talents. Wayne Kusy is an artist.

Now, close your eyes a moment and picture an artist at work. . . What did you see? A person with a brush and little pots of paint painting a picture on a big piece of paper? A lot of artists paint on paper, canvas, wood, and even walls. Others make sculptures from rock or clay. But Wayne Kusy doesn't use paint or clay to make his expressive creations. He uses hundreds of thousands of toothpicks to make scale models of ocean liners.

A scale model is much smaller than the real thing it looks like, but it has all the same parts and proportions. A scale model is the real thing shrunk down to much smaller size, like a dollhouse or a toy airplane.

Wayne has been making toothpick ship models ever since he was ten years old. He completed his first model when he was in the fifth grade. It was an art-class project. That first ship was made of 3,000 toothpicks. Later he built a scale model of the famous ocean liner *Titanic*. The real *Titanic* was nearly as long as three football fields. Wayne's much smaller finished model was ten feet long and took 75,000 toothpicks to build.

Wayne is famous for accuracy and attention to detail. He works with boxes of toothpicks, cans of wood glue, wire cutters, a ruler, and paint to make exact replicas, down to the tiniest, most exquisite details. That includes portholes, stairways, and lifeboats complete with teeny oars for rowing.

As Wayne continued working through the years, his models kept growing in size. His biggest project of all was a scale-model replica of the *Queen Mary*, a passenger ship even larger than the *Titanic*. Wayne's model consists of nearly a million toothpicks held together with thirty gallons of wood glue. He worked from two to three hours a night for eight years in his Chicago apartment to finish it.

His completed model was 25 feet long from stem to stern. When an art museum wanted to exhibit his *Queen Mary*, Wayne had to take it apart to get it out of the apartment. It came out in six separate sections that took four hours to put back together in the museum.

Wayne Kusy is a special kind of creator. In the art world, he's known as an outsider artist. That means he never went to art school. Like other outsider artists, Wayne is self-taught. One day he just picked up a box of toothpicks and some glue and set to work, and he's been creating art ever since.

Like Wayne Kusy with his toothpicks, outsider artists often use unusual, unlikely materials. Some work with recycled trash. Outsider artists have used scraps of paper, chunks of cardboard, burnt matchsticks, old chewed chewing gum, and hunks of scrap metal.

Even old bottles have been turned into works of art by one of these outsider artists. Her name is Tressa Prisbrey. That's a hard name to pronounce, so we'll just call her what everyone else called her: Grandma.

Grandma's Bottle Village is in Simi Valley, a city in southern California. The village consists of fifteen separate structures, all made of bottles—tens of thousands of bottles. Bottle Village has a history that goes back more than fifty years, all the way back to 1956. That's when Grandma began working on it, at the age of sixty. She didn't finish her Bottle Village until 1981, when she was seventy-five years old. That's right, Grandma worked on her creation for 25 years!

Like Wayne Kusy, Grandma Prisbrey was a self-taught artist. She was also a collector. One day she drove out to the county dump and started picking up bottles that others had thrown away. After that, she kept returning to the dump to bring back more and more bottles. What should she do with all those bottles? Grandma decided to make walls of bottles held together with concrete.

Pretty soon the walls became a building and then another building and then another, with wishing wells and walkways running between them. Through the years Grandma added all sorts of other objects to her village, including dolls' heads, TV screens, and automobile headlights, all recovered from the dump. Grandma Prisbrey died in 1988, but her recycled creation lives on.

Grandma's Bottle Village has been declared a historical treasure by the County of Ventura, by the state of California, and by the United States government.

Why did Grandma Prisbrey spend 25 years creating her outsider art masterpiece? Her Bottle Village didn't make her rich. No, Grandma said, she did not make her artwork for money. She built her Bottle Village for the fun of it.

Charlie Lucas is another artist who spends lots of time at the dump. But instead of bottles, Charlie looks for scrap metal to recycle into artistic creations. He makes sculptures and statues out of the metal that others have thrown away. That's why they call him "the Tin Man."

Like Wayne Kusy, Charlie Lucas began making things at a very young age. Charlie's father was an expert auto mechanic who taught his son how to take an automobile engine apart and put it back together again.

When Charlie got older he began collecting old scrap metal from scrap yards and dumps and turning it into sculptures and statues. Some of them are huge. Charlie's yard in Prattville, Alabama, has metal sculptures of enormous birds and prehistoric dinosaurs, and even a big rusty handmade airplane.

People from all around the world buy Charlie's artworks and exhibit his sculptures in museums. Charlie Lucas has become a famous and highly-praised artist. But he doesn't think of his statues and sculptures as serious works of art. Instead, he calls them his toys. "I've been making toys since I was a kid," the Tin Man says. "If I called them anything else I wouldn't know what I was talking about."

Outsider artists are usually playful artists. They have loads of fun doing what they do.

But some are more serious about their work. They see their creations as significant—as serious and important. Nek Chand is one of these serious outsider artists. When he was a child, Nek imagined an entire kingdom full of kings and queens, townspeople, and all sorts of animals, real and make-believe, living peacefully together in a lovely forest.

The forest was in northern India, where Nek grew up. When he was 27, Nek saw a chance to turn his dream into a work of art. Near where he lived was a large forest, a nature reserve that was protected by the government. Also nearby were the ruins of several villages that had been knocked down to make way for the huge new modern city of Chandigarh. Nek began gathering bits and pieces of the knocked-down villages. He collected chunks of rock, glass, pottery, metal, and wood that no one else wanted. These would be his art materials.

He took these materials into the forest and started turning them into statues of the figures in his dream. No one was allowed to build anything in the forest. The government forbid it. But Nek kept building his dream among the trees anyway, secretly, hidden away from everyone else.

Some of Nek's statues are arranged in groups to make a significant point. One group of Indian women is shown gathering water from a stream. In some parts of India, fresh water is hard to find. Nek wanted this group of statue women to make a very important and relevant point about Indian life: that fresh water must be carefully conserved and used with care.

As the years passed, Nek kept working. Only his wife and a few close friends, who all kept his secret, knew about Nek's growing creation. After sixteen years of collecting and building, Nek had created two thousand colorful dream figures.

Then something unexpected happened. A crew of government workers accidentally stumbled upon it. Imagine how they must have felt, walking through a wild forest and suddenly finding themselves surrounded by thousands of strangely beautiful statues made of bits and pieces of the ruined villages. Nek's secret kingdom was a secret no more.

Word spread quickly, and people from nearby Chandigarh rushed to the forest to see Nek's dream-world of statues. They saw statues of real and make-believe animals gathered together. They saw statues of kings and queens and princes and princesses. They saw groups of statue dancers who looked like they were really dancing and statue musicians who almost seemed to be playing their instruments. And they saw the group of statue women collecting precious fresh water from a stream.

Those who saw Nek's creations were amazed at his imagination and skill. The statues' clothes were made of broken pots and shiny glass. Some of the heads were made from bicycle seats, and the hair on the heads was real human hair that Nek had collected from local barbershops. Nek could discover a use for just about anything that other people saw as useless.

At first the government threatened to have the forbidden statues taken away.

But many people protested, and finally Nek's kingdom was allowed to remain in the forest reserve. It was officially named the Rock Garden, and ever since then the government has paid Nek a salary to keep adding to it. Today, his Rock Garden has more than 5,000 sculptures, and people from all around the world come to admire Nek Chand's kingdom of outsider art.

Toothpicks, bottles, tins, and rocks? Artists like Wayne, Grandma, Charlie, and Nek see ordinary materials in brand new ways. And then they use these everyday objects to create beauty and art that amaze us all.

Hannah Hopper's Hunt for Rules and Laws

BY GLENN HANSEN

All the students in Miss Garcia's fourth-grade social studies class sat up straight in their seats. Twenty-nine hands picked up twenty-nine pencils. As their teacher spoke, they all wrote the same two words in their notebooks: *Rules* and *Laws*.

"Here is your homework assignment for the weekend," Miss Garcia told them. "You are going to do some observing. I am going to ask you to look and listen and learn."

"Another challenge," thought Hannah Hopper. Hannah loved challenges. She sat in the row next to the big window that looked out on the playground. She thought of what Miss Garcia had predicted on the first day of school: "By the end of the school year, each and every one of you will become a keen and alert observer of the world around you."

Last month Hannah and her classmates had spent a weekend looking for all the ways in which people cooperate and help one another. This month their focus would be rules and laws. Miss Garcia explained the difference between the two. First, she explained what rules were. "In places like your school and home there are rules to live by," she said. "Don't run in the halls is a rule in our school. Be in bed by a certain time is a rule at home. Rules are made by groups of people, like school boards and families."

Then Miss Garcia explained what laws were. "Out in our neighborhood and town, there are laws for everyone to follow. 'Always wear your seat belt in the car' is a law. So is 'Don't litter.' Laws are made by elected leaders. Elected officials in our nation's capitol, Washington, D.C., make the laws for our nation. It is every citizen's duty to follow the rules and obey the laws. People who break rules or laws face consequences.

"Now," Miss Garcia continued, "each of you will make a list of the rules and laws that you observe this weekend. As usual, the student with the longest list wins the mystery prize. And don't forget, you must discover these rules and laws for yourself. And one more thing, class. For this particular assignment, don't just pay attention to what you see. Also pay attention to what you do *not* see."

Richard Jenkins raised his hand and asked Miss Garcia what she meant by "what you do *not* see."

"You will have to figure that out for yourself, Richard. That goes for all of you," Miss Garcia added. "Good luck."

Hannah looked over at Richard Jenkins. He almost always had the longest list, no matter what Miss Garcia had them look for. But that just made Hannah try harder. "Maybe this time I, Hannah Hopper, will win the mystery prize," she thought.

Hannah was waiting for the bus after school when she spotted Richard Jenkins with his notebook open. He was looking up at the **NO PARKING except buses** sign. "Ah-ha," Hannah thought, "another law."

Hannah added it to her list. Wow, she already had ten items: six rules and four laws. "But I bet Richard has even more," Hannah thought. You had to be a super-keen observer if you expected to beat Richard Jenkins.

When Hannah arrived at the house, she found her mom in her home office working at her computer. Hannah told her about the assignment.

"Rules and laws?" Mom said. "That's interesting. Want some help?"

"Thanks, Mom," Hannah said, "but we have to do this all on our own."

"Ah, yes," Mom remembered. "So you can become—what is it Miss Garcia always says? 'A keen and alert observer.' Right?"

"Right," Hannah said.

"I like Miss Garcia," Mom said.

"Me too, Mom," Hannah agreed.

Next morning after breakfast, Hannah asked permission to walk to town in search of more rules and laws. "Fine," Dad said, "as long as you take your little sister along. Jenny has overdue library books."

Jenny was a year younger than Hannah, and sometimes she acted like Little-Miss-Know-It-All. But only sometimes, so Hannah didn't complain. "OK, Jen, let's go," she said.

It was a warm day with just a few fluffy clouds in the sky. At the corner of Sixth and Walnut, Hannah stopped and opened her notebook.

"Are you writing more rules and laws?" Jenny asked.

"Right," Hannah replied, pointing to the sign on the post office wall that read: **NO SKATEBOARDS ON SIDEWALK**.

The library was just across the street. Walking in through the big automatic doors, Hannah immediately noticed how the noise level dropped. Suddenly it was so much quieter. "Ah," thought Hannah, opening her notebook, "the library quiet rule." Then, as Jenny paid her fine to the lady at the circulation desk, Hannah added the rule about library fines to her ever-growing list.

Back outside, Hannah and Jenny stopped in front of Lawson's Shoe Store. Jenny watched as Hannah peered into the store window. At the front of the store, Mr. Lawson pulled a pair of tennis shoes from a box for a woman try on. At the back of the store, a tall man who had bought a pair of cowboy boots handed Mrs. Lawson some money, and she rang up the sale on the cash register.

"Nothing here," Hannah decided, turning away. "No rules or laws in action in Lawson's." But then Hannah turned back as Mrs. Lawson handed the tall man his change and a receipt. "Wait a minute," Hannah said. "Taxes."

"Texas?" Jenny asked.

"No, Jen, not the state of Texas. *Taxes*. T-A-X-E-S. In our state, the law says you have to pay taxes when you buy something in a store. The tax gets added on to the price of whatever you buy. It's one way our state raises money."

"Oh, sure, I knew all that," Jenny said quickly.

"Are you sure?" Hannah asked.

Jenny looked down at the sidewalk. "Well, maybe not exactly, I guess." Then Jenny smiled up at her big sister. "But I know now, don't I?" Jenny asked.

"Yes, now you truly do know," Hannah smiled back.

"So maybe I could help you out. Wait, you've got to do this on your own, right? OK, but what if I just point?" Jenny asked.

"I suppose just pointing would be all right," Hannah said.

So Jenny gestured across the street where three boys were riding their bikes. Hannah right away noticed the same thing Jenny had noticed: the boys were all wearing bike helmets.

Jenny looked pleased with herself. "I'm on my way to being a keen and alert observer of rules and laws, don't you think?"

"Absolutely," Hannah grinned.

By the time Monday morning arrived, Jenny had filled seven whole pages of her notebook with rules and laws she had seen in action that weekend. But would her list be long enough to win the mystery prize? Hannah added her notebook to the growing pile on Miss Garcia's desk.

Social studies was the final subject of the day. By then, Miss Garcia had looked over all twenty-nine lists and was ready to announce the winner. When she called Richard Jenkins up to the front of the room, Hannah was not surprised. But then she called Hannah up too. Amazed, Hannah took her place next to Richard facing the class. They both looked puzzled, and so did the rest of the class, until Miss Garcia announced that there had been a tie.

"A tie?," Richard said, disappointed.

"A tie!" Hannah cried, excited.

"Now," said Miss Garcia, handing Richard and Hannah their notebooks, "let's see if we can break this tie between these two keen and alert observers. Look around for a rule or law that you might have missed. And remember all the things I told you last Friday. You have one minute, starting now."

Hannah felt butterflies flutter in her stomach as she looked all around, from Richard to Miss Garcia to the other twenty-seven students at their desks to the blackboard to the class pet, Eugene, a hamster running on the wheel in his cage.

"No rules or laws here," Hannah thought.

Then she looked out the big window to the empty playground and across the street to where a woman in a baseball cap walked her dog on a leash. There was a law in action: 'You must always have your dog on a leash.' But Hannah could only sigh. She already had the leash law written out on the list in her notebook.

Then Hannah's gaze shifted to the empty playground, and something Miss Garcia had said last Friday came back to her: "Also pay attention to what you do *not* see."

Until that moment Hannah had not known what Miss Garcia meant. Now she understood. The playground was empty. There were no dogs there. "Of course," Hannah said, and excitedly wrote in her notebook.

"Time's up," Miss Garcia said. "What have you got?"

All Richard could do was shake his head sadly and say, "Nothing."

"Here," Hannah said, handing over her notebook.

Miss Garcia smiled as she read aloud what Hannah had just written: "There are no dogs allowed on the playground."

"It's a school rule, right?" Hannah asked.

"Correct," Miss Garcia said. "Congratulations, Hannah." Richard shook her hand, Miss Garcia awarded Hannah the mystery prize, and the class gave her a big round of applause.

When Hannah got home that afternoon, her little sister was waiting in the kitchen. "So," Jenny asked, "did you win?"

"I did," Hannah said, smiling.

"I knew you would," Jenny said, and gave her big sister a big hug. "So, show me the mystery prize."

Hannah pulled a blue box with a red ribbon from her backpack and set it on the kitchen table. Jenny slid off the ribbon and opened the box. Inside, on a black velvet lining, was a big magnifying glass with a black handle and rim.

"Ooh!" Jenny said, picking it up with great care. She trained the thick glass on her fingertips and leaned in close. "Wow, you can actually see your fingerprints, every little curve and line. Mr. Hester says my fingerprints are unique. That means they're different from everyone else's. I bet you didn't know that."

Mr. Hester was Jenny's third grade science teacher. Hannah said that actually she did know that, but Jenny didn't hear her. All of Jenny's attention was on the magnifying glass and the view it gave Jenny of her unique fingerprints.

"Well," Hannah said, "looks like I'll have to tell Miss Garcia that we have another keen and alert observer in the family."

The Boy Who Stopped Time

BY ANTHONY TABOR

No matter how much fun he was having, every night at 7:30, when the clock on the living room wall went *ding-dong*, Julian had to go to bed.

One summer evening, just before bedtime, Julian asked his mom if he could stay up late to watch a special TV show. "No, Julian," she said. "You need your rest more than you need that show. When the big hand gets to the six, it's off to bed with you." She left the living room to tuck in his little sister, AnnaRose.

Julian watched the clock's pendulum swing back and forth until the big hand slid past the five. Then he went to the window. Outside, his father was piling stones in the yard. And from his sister's bedroom he heard his mother begin a lullaby. Julian suddenly had a wonderful idea. He pushed a chair beneath the clock, the climbed up and opened the clock's face. He took a deep breath . . . and stopped the pendulum. A strange hush fell over the house.

He tiptoed down the hall to his sister's room. There in the shadows was his mom, leaning over AnnaRose's crib. Her mouth was open as if she were singing, and AnnaRose was smiling up at her. Everything looked perfectly normal, except his mom and his sister were both as still and as quiet as statues. Julian backed out of the room, amazed at what he had done, and ran outside.

He found his dad with arms outstretched by the rock pile, his eyes fixed on a big rock he had just thrown. Julian called to him but got no reply. Looking at his dad made Julian feel guilty. He had not intended to have *everything* stop, only the clock. Maybe he should start the clock again, even though he would have to go to bed.

But on the way back to the house he thought of not having to go to bed. The more he thought about it the better he liked the idea. If he didn't start the clock he never had to go to bed again. So . . . instead of going inside, he walked slowly around the house, fascinated by the eerie stillness.

Down by the creek that edged their land, he encountered a magnificent buck deer. It was twice his height, with a huge rack of antlers. Julian had to use a stepladder from the shed to reach its back. Up there he felt like the king of all he saw, and wished he could make the deer move from the creek and race over the countryside. He looked at his house and his father by the stone pile. He could still go anywhere and do anything he wanted. He decided to take his bike up the driveway to the main road, where he was strictly forbidden to go.

Before leaving, he stopped at the house, gave his mom a secret kiss good-bye, and took some cookies for the trip. He pedaled fearlessly out onto the main road and didn't stop until he was almost a mile away, at the first intersection. He had never been this far on his own before. Julian stopped at the library. It was still hard to read by himself. He wished Miss Bruning, the children's librarian, could help as she had many times before.

He went to the movie theater, but the picture wasn't moving, and the silence and stillness crept into him. He felt sleepy and dozed off. Julian didn't know how long he had slept because when he woke everything was exactly the same. Then he remembered how he had stopped the clock so he wouldn't have to go to sleep.

Listening to the silence within himself, Julian pedaled to the town park. He looked at all the children frozen in their play. Now his feeling of silence started to become a feeling of sadness, and he knew that he wanted to go home.

He took the back road home. Cows and horses stood motionless in the fields, and high above, an airplane hung in the sky. He was very tired when he arrived and very happy to find everything waiting for him just as he had left it.

He put his bike away, went inside, peeked in at his mom, climbed up on the chair, and started the clock pendulum swinging again. His mother's lullaby began again. He got down and silently returned the chair to its place. The lullaby ended, the clock went *ding-dong*, and his mother said, "It's time, Julian."

He took one last look out the window. His father was throwing another stone on the pile. Down by the creek, the deer had gone, and over the meadow honeybees gathered nectar in the evening sun. Julian smiled to himself and quietly went to bed.

Abraham Lincoln: A Man for All the People

BY MYRA COHN LIVINGSTON

A man for all the people,
A man who stood up tall,
Abe Lincoln spoke of justice
And liberty for all.

Born in a log cabin
Work was what he knew,
Helped chop trees, plant corn, split logs.
Abe just grew and grew.

Abe moved to Indiana,
Abe moved to Illinois.
Always spent time reading
Since he was a boy.

Settled in New Salem
When he was twenty-one,
Worked a while at clerking.
Abe's manhood had begun.

Tried to run for office,
Learned how to survey,
Wrestled and debated,
Kept learning every day.

Abe Lincoln was a lawyer,
Respected all the laws.
Rode the circuit fighting
For every human cause.

Moved again to Springfield.
People liked his looks.
Married Mary, had four sons,
Kept on reading books.

Abe went into politics,
Called slavery a blight,
Debated Stephen Douglas
With faith that "Rights makes Might."

Abe was fun and witty,
Abe was moody, sad;
Spoke up for the good things,
Spoke against the bad.

Abe Lincoln ran for president.
He heard his country's call
Believing that "the people's will"
Should be the law for all.

Abe moved into the White House.
He sought equality.
He said, "All persons held as slaves
Henceforward shall be free."

Abe Lincoln was our president
All through the Civil War.
He knew the "fiery trial" ahead,
What men were fighting for.

Abe Lincoln spoke at Gettysburg.
He wrote a nation free
"Shall not perish from the earth."
Abe loved democracy.

"Fondly, do we hope," he said,
"Fervently do we pray
That this mighty scourge of war
May speedily pass away."

Abe Lincoln led his generals,
And prayed the war would cease.
"Bind up the nation's wounds," he said.
"Cherish a lasting peace."

Abe knew he was in danger.
He dreamed that he was dead.
He went to see a play one night.
Booth shot him in the head.

Abe Lincoln was a strong man
True to the people's will.
Tall, like his marble statue,
He sits among us still.

A man for all the people,
A man who stood up tall.
Abe Lincoln honored justice
And liberty for all.

Martin's Dream

BY ROBERT KAUSAL

How do you feel when someone treats you unfairly? Do you get angry and yell? Do you cry? Or do you turn around and walk away? We all respond differently to being mistreated, but the pain of an injustice hurts everyone just the same.

It was this pain of injustice that started the civil rights movement in the 1950s. Civil rights are the basic rights of all citizens to be treated fairly and equally. Many people had different ideas about how to achieve civil rights, but one man's dream became the driving force behind this movement. That man was Martin Luther King, Jr. On August 28, 1963, he and other civil rights leaders organized a march to the nation's capital. The highlight of the demonstration would be Martin's "I Have a Dream" speech. People wept and cheered as they listened to his vision of a better America.

Martin Luther King delivered his famous speech on the steps of the Lincoln Memorial. He started by telling his audience that even though President Abraham Lincoln had freed black slaves a hundred year earlier that blacks were still not free. He said that we are still bound by the "chains of discrimination" and live "on a lonely island of poverty."

Martin first experienced poverty and discrimination in his hometown of Atlanta, Georgia. It was there that he had to sit in the balcony if he wanted to watch a movie.

It was there that he had to use a separate water fountain "For Colored Only." And it was there that he had to give up his seat on a bus for a white person. He later said, "It was the angriest I have ever been in my life." But his anger did not get the best of him. His father, Martin Luther King, Sr. taught him to be dignified and not show his anger. And his mother always told him, "You're as good as anyone." It was this strong family support that helped form Martin's character.

Now, on the steps of the Lincoln Memorial, in front of more than 200,000 people and millions more watching on TV, Martin Luther King spoke about his dream of equality.

"I have a dream!" he cried. "I have a dream that one day on the red hills of Georgia, sons of former slaves and sons of former slave owners will be able to sit down together at the table of brotherhood. I have a dream that one day even the state of Mississippi, a state sweltering with the heat of injustice, sweltering with the heat of oppression, will be transformed into an oasis of freedom and justice. I have a dream that my four little children will one day live in a nation where they will not be judged by the color of their skin but by the content of their character. I have a dream today!"

The crowd was moved by Martin's words. His dream had touched the heart of a nation. Everyone knew it was up to all of us to make this dream a reality.

The following year, Martin was present as President Johnson signed into law the Civil Rights Act of 1964. It would end segregation in public places. The same year *Time* magazine named Martin Luther King Jr. "Man of the Year." He would also win the Nobel Peace Prize.

While the civil rights movement continued to make progress over the next few years, sadly it would suffer its worst setback in 1968. In that year, on the balcony of a Memphis, Tennessee motel, Martin Luther King, Jr. was shot and killed. People everywhere mourned the fallen leader. Many people were confused. Some people responded to the news with violence.

However, most people responded to this tragedy with a determination to make his dream a reality. Martin's dream would never die. His vision and hope for a better world lives on in his words and his actions. In 1986, the United States officially named Martin's Birthday, January 15, a national holiday.